D0049109

DRAMA IN
THE BAHAMAS

DRAMA IN THE BAHAMAS

MUHAMMAD ALI'S LAST FIGHT

DAVE HANNIGAN

SPORTS
PUBLISHING

Sports Publishing books may be purchased in bulk at special discounts for sales promotion, corporate gifts, fund-raising, or educational purposes. Special editions can also be created to specifications. For details, contact the Special Sales Department, Sports Publishing, 307 West 36th Street, 11th Floor, New York, NY 10018 or sportspubbooks@ skyhorsepublishing.com.

Sports Publishing® is a registered trademark of Skyhorse Publishing, Inc.®, a Delaware corporation.

Visit our website at www.sportspubbooks.com.

10 9 8 7 6 5 4 3 2 1

Library of Congress Cataloging-in-Publication Data is available on file.

Cover design by Tom Lau
Cover photo credit: Associated Press

ISBN: 987-1-61321-898-3
Ebook ISBN: 978-1-61321-899-0

Printed in the United States of America

Contents

To the memory of my mother, Theresa

Prologue

As DEACON OF THE CHURCH of God in Norwich, Jamaica, eighty-four-year-old Canute Lambert hosted an early morning prayer meeting in the chapel every Saturday. Just after six a.m. on October 28, 2006, Lambert arrived at his place of worship to prepare for the arrival of his most devoted parishioners. Immediately, he noticed some sort of large object at the top of the steps to the entrance. At first, from a distance, he figured it was a garbage bag discarded there by somebody the previous night.

Beginning his ascent, however, Lambert recognized a trail of crimson tracking beneath his feet. Looking up, he was close enough to see what lay at the top of the church steps was not refuse but a body. "It looked like a human being," he said later. When he bent over the corpse, even with four gaping wounds in its head, he knew immediately who it was. Lambert had known Trevor Berbick from the day he was born. He had watched him grow up, leave the island, become world famous and return, only to die in a pool of blood, a $100 bill lying beside him, yards from his home.

Within hours, news of Berbick's death was flashing up on websites and newspapers across the world. Almost every headline described the former heavyweight champion as "the last man to fight Muhammad Ali." His calling card in history.

CHAPTER ONE
What Happens in Vegas

I can't represent the Muslims again until I quit sports. I spoke with the Honorable Elijah Muhammad, and he told me, "If boxing's in your blood, get it out." I've got a few more things to do before I can get it out of my blood, about four more fights. First is the one with James Ellis down in Houston, and the last one will be with Frazier. Then I will be free to represent the Muslims again.

Muhammad Ali, June 22, 1971

BORN ON WESTMON ISLAND IN Iceland in 1944, Sig Rogich was five when his parents moved to America, eventually settling in Henderson, Nevada. For a financially struggling family it was a fortuitous time to arrive, as nearby Las Vegas was undergoing its first prolonged boom. Rogich worked his way through high school and college busing tables at the casinos and doing stints as a hotel bell-boy along the strip. Before turning thirty, he founded what became the state's largest advertising agency, made his first million, and was such an influential player around town he once helped Frank Sinatra obtain a gambling license.

Walking through the doors of the state building in Las Vegas on the morning of December 29, 1980, Rogich cut a debonair figure, wearing his usual tailored Italian suit and expensive loafers, and carrying the title of chairman of the Nevada State Athletic Commission. For six years he'd served on the five-member body charged with sanctioning boxing matches and licensing fighters. Since Vegas had essentially become the world capital of the sport in that time, this made the committee arguably the most powerful quintet in the game.

The reach of their impact and significance of their decision-making was hammered home to Rogich when he saw that more than fifty journalists had arrived for the meeting. He knew why they had come. He understood why editors had sent them from all over America. He realized this was no ordinary meeting. On this day he was tasked with presiding over a hearing to decide whether Muhammad Ali would ever climb through the ropes of a boxing ring again.

In the nearly three months that had passed since the thirty-eight-year-old former champion had been resoundingly defeated by Larry Holmes in an improvised arena in the car park of Caesars Palace, his fistic future had hung in the balance. It had been put there very firmly by Rogich's own comments to the press in the aftermath of that bout.

"I believe we should retire a great champion for his safety and the integrity of the sport," said the chairman of the commission back in October. "He demonstrated after the fight he should not be fighting again."

The troubling manner of Ali's loss that night of October 2, 1980, the sheer lifelessness of his performance, and the disturbing sight of him absorbing so much savage punishment was, many would say belatedly, forcing the commission's hand. The jig, finally, appeared up.

"Ain't this something?" said Ali, as he was corralled by reporters on the way into the hearing. "One bad day on the job and they want to fire me."

If his quip made for characteristically good copy, the case against him was overwhelming. Aside from the damning evidence provided by the ten torturous rounds of the Holmes beatdown, a horror show only ended by trainer Angelo Dundee refusing to let him answer the bell for the eleventh, there were other serious issues to consider. Ali had used thyroid medication before the contest (to excess, he himself would admit), and taken painkillers immediately after it, crucially before the mandatory post-fight urinalysis had even been conducted.

There was then a surfeit of available reasons why the commission seemed bound to ensure the sixtieth fight of Ali's pro career was also going to be his last. Indeed, recognizing the weakness of his position, and knowing the lay of the land from Rogich's public statements, Ali's attorneys had tried to preempt the hearing. In a letter dated December 19, they offered to surrender his license in Nevada, a gesture that would make the adjudication moot and, more importantly for the boxer's future prospects, not force other states to take their lead from the most influential commission in the sport and effectively retire him.

Rogich and his colleagues didn't buy this gambit. They were determined to wield their power to call a halt to perhaps the greatest career the sport had ever seen. They countered to his lawyers that Ali's offer to surrender the license meant nothing if they refused to accept it. And, after a vote, that's exactly what they decided to do.

So then the hearing began in earnest. A fight film was produced of the Holmes bout, and Ali's attorneys—Michael Phenner, Michael Conway, and Niels Pearson—began arguing the case on behalf of their client.

Befitting a commission that usually didn't draw a big crowd, the meeting was held in a small room. However, so many people had shoehorned into it for this case that it soon began to get hot and clammy. As the proceedings dragged on, Ali grew visibly bored by the lawyerly back and forth. He could be seen doodling away on pieces of paper—that is, until he spotted a pair of kids in the public gallery.

Che and Kwasi Cunningham had been brought along by their mother. In this pair, Ali had found himself the perfect distraction from the labyrinthine business at hand. Beckoning them forward to his seat, he began entertaining his newfound audience with magic tricks.

"I'm sitting there watching this and thinking, 'My God!'" said Patricia Cunningham. "Here's Muhammad Ali entertaining my kids while the commission is deciding whether or not he can fight. There were all these media and cameras there, and Ali didn't even look at them. He was just having such a good time with the boys. I'll never forget it."

Ali asked the Cunningham lads if they were hungry. They were. So he dispatched a member of his entourage to a nearby McDonalds to bring the boys back some food. Soon, the thick smell of French fries wafted through the overheated room, adding a unique flavor to an already sticky atmosphere.

Although it might have looked as if he wasn't paying attention, Ali clearly knew what was going on. The morning session had not gone his way, and he used the interval to inform the press he was already considering going down other legal avenues.

"I've set aside two million dollars if this goes to court. I don't feel humiliated, but this is silly," said Ali. "I'll take this to the highest court if I have to. They can't retire me without giving me a chance to prove myself again. Look at all the fighters who were knocked out cold—Earnie Shavers, Ken Norton, John Tate, George Foreman, Joe Frazier—they never tried to retire them. I'm not just some ordinary Negro off the street. I'm the most controversial fighter in history. They can't railroad me. We're going to make this a world case. This is going to be a good rumble…bigger than the fight."

The commission definitely wanted to stop Ali fighting again in Nevada. But, it also definitely needed to avoid the type of costly and embarrassing litigation during which the spotlight would inevitably fall on how and why Rogich and his cohorts had considered Ali fit to fight Holmes in the first place, especially after a two-year hiatus from the ring. That scandalous decision hung like a dark cloud over the entire proceeding.

By the same token, any move to a federal court by Ali's camp would also necessitate a rigorous independent investigation of the fighter's health that would surely end his hopes of lacing up gloves anywhere ever again. For the sake of both parties then, a face-saving compromise was badly needed.

A solution was found when Rogich met Gene Kilroy, Ali's business manager/facilitator, in the men's room during a break in the afternoon session; the two struck an informal deal. The commission would, after all, accept Ali's surrender of his license, and the fighter would, in return, promise never to apply to fight in the state again.

"I think everyone had a chance to make their point," said Rogich, after announcing the decision, demonstrating a talent for spin that he would later put to good use in the presidential election campaigns of Ronald Reagan and George H.W. Bush. "We all must give and take a little. For health and safety reasons, the state acted properly. The decision was best for all parties concerned. This hearing wasn't held to embarrass Ali."

Obviously pleased with the deal, Ali shook hands with Rogich and then delivered his own verdict to the cameras.

"They think I can't fight anymore," he said. "According to my last performance, I don't blame them. I don't have too many fights left. But I didn't want to go out being retired. I want to be free to make my own decision. If I stop, it's because I want to stop. Nobody's going to make me stop."

And that was the bigger issue at stake. Now that the Nevada State Athletic Commission, for all its presumed power and influence, had effectively washed its hands of Ali, who then possessed the power to make him stop? Who had the wherewithal to save him from himself, especially when there were always going to be others intent on helping him to keep going, no matter the increasingly obvious personal and physical toll it was exacting on him?

The very next morning's *New York Times* carried an item about him possibly fighting in Madison Square Garden as soon as February. Within days, there was speculation about him applying for a license to compete in Hawaii. In both cases, the name of the English heavyweight prospect and European champion John L. Gardner was mentioned as the most likely candidate for his sixty-first outing. Talk of that bout had preceded the Vegas hearing.

Indeed, eleven days before the showdown in Vegas, Ali had touched down in London to promote *Freedom Road*, NBC's historical mini-series in which he played Gideon Jackson, a former soldier and Civil War veteran who becomes a United States senator. Immaculately turned out in a suit and tie, rain mac draped over one arm, small suitcase in the other, he shadowboxed for some young fans at Heathrow Airport and signed umpteen autographs. Yet, some of the photographers capturing his arrival felt he was a more subdued version of his normally effervescent self.

Prior to the premiere on British television, Ali took a suite at the Dorchester Hotel where he seemed to spend more time talking about his desire to continue boxing, rather than extolling the virtues of acting alongside luminaries like Kris Kristofferson.

"If I am not allowed to fight John L. Gardner, I will call all my people and all my fans to march from Harlem to Manhattan, and from the Washington ghettoes to the Capitol," said Ali. "We are going to march all over America. I am going to shake up the whole country."

That threat was delivered with a glint in his eye, and mock-seriousness in his voice. And, at one point, he sounded refreshingly stoic about his future. "I don't need boxing. What you thought you needed yesterday, you are sometimes shown you don't need tomorrow."

Yet, for all that, he couldn't help but return again and again during his time in England to the lust to continue fighting.

"If you judged all fighters on one performance, you would have to stop a whole lot of them from fighting. Let me fight Gardner and I say that if I lose or look bad beating him, I will get out of boxing. I want to go on because I am the only man in the history of the sport with the chance of winning the heavyweight title for a fourth time. I shall be old in a year or two."

During his brief stay in London, Ali was typically busy. He visited the House of Commons at the invitation of Martin Stevens, Conservative MP for Fulham, and there was the inevitable parade of visitors to his hotel room. A then up-and-coming Irish actor named Liam Neeson was among those granted an audience.

"We were up in his suite and I remember children being there," said Neeson. "Ali, he's famous for it, went straight for the kids and we were all ignored for a few minutes. Eventually, we formed a semi-circle and he was coming around, shaking hands with everybody. My knees were genuinely shaking. You're going to meet your hero, and I thought, 'I have to say something to him because I'll never get the chance in my life again.' And, as he came up to me, I just went, 'Man, I love you!'"

Ali also resumed his professional relationship with the legendary English broadcaster, Michael Parkinson. In a lively appearance on Parkinson's chat show, Ali was forced to defend his desire to continue fighting.

Parkinson: You've seen the shambling wrecks that go around, you see them at every boxing occasion. And what people are frightened of is they don't want that to happen to you.

Ali: What, to be a shambling wreck?

Parkinson: That's right.

Ali: I'm a long ways from a shambling wreck.

Parkinson: Oh, I'm not suggesting you are now. I'm saying that's what they're frightened might happen.

Ali: Let me tell you why they're frightened. Some people can see farther than others. Some people are pressed with limitations....

If Ali appeared in good fettle while jousting with Parkinson, problems arose during two other interviews he recorded for BBC radio. In the first he recited a poem about how he would win any rematch with Larry Holmes, the usual Ali shtick except listeners struggled to make out what he was saying. In the second, his speech was even more slurred and, as a result, the BBC decided not to broadcast it.

"It was very sad that so much of what history's greatest fighter said was unintelligible," said the BBC's official statement on the matter.

In the face of that rather compelling and objective evidence that all was almost certainly not right, one English reporter asked Ali whether he was punch drunk. "I have heard about people being punch drunk but I do not feel drunk. When you get as great as me, people always look for some sort of downfall."

He need not have worried unduly. There were plenty of others out there wanting to afford him the chance to continue boxing, wherever and whenever that might happen.

Despite the embarrassment with the BBC and the licensing setback in Las Vegas, Ali began 1981 determined to get back in the ring against Gardner, with the Neal Blaisdell Center in Honolulu in April the most likely time and place.

"If I stop it's because I want to stop," said Ali. "Nobody can make me stop."

That was true. That also became his mantra as opposition to his intentions mounted.

On January 7, he was in Honolulu taking the physical examination necessary for him to be licensed to fight there. At a meeting of the Hawaiian Boxing Commission five days later, Dr. Richard You testified that, in his opinion, Ali was fit to fight if he addressed some health issues before climbing into the ring. He was deemed overweight (twenty-three pounds heavier than when he fought Holmes), had less than normal blood sugar, and minor problems with his kidneys. Otherwise, the fighter was in "good physical condition."

However, Hawaii managed to wriggle off the hook on a technicality. The commission voted 3-2 to defer Ali's application for a license until it had received written clarification from the Nevada State Athletic Commission clarifying his exact status as a fighter there. Essentially, they were trying to buy themselves time. A subsequent phone call confirmed the truth of the earlier assertion by Harold Smith, chairman of Muhammad Ali Professional Sports, a company set up in 1977 to promote events using the Ali brand, that he had merely "surrendered" his license in Las Vegas.

The officials were stalling, because five days after the hearing Ali would turn thirty-nine and Hawaii had a law preventing any fighters over the age of thirty-eight from being licensed, thereby rendering any future meeting on the topic moot.

After the decision was announced, Smith had a roaring match with Ed Kalahiki, chairman of the commission and the person who had been the swing vote on the issue. The fact that the Governor of Hawaii, George R. Ariyoshi, had appointed Robert R. Lee to the commission just an hour before the meeting was something the Ali camp regarded as "mighty suspicious."

"The governor never told me to kill the fight, but I think he knew how I felt about it," said Lee, two decades later. "Ali was deteriorating and people just wanted to use him and make money off of him. We didn't know then about his Parkinson's disease, of course, but you could tell he'd already had enough."

Incensed, Smith announced his intention to sue the state for an amount of money large enough to deter others from denying his man the right to fight.

"This is a sham," said Smith. "I feel more sadly for the people of Hawaii and Sam Ichinose [the local promoter of the proposed fight] than I do for Ali. Ali's big enough. He can go anywhere. It's Hawaii's loss, not his."

Whatever the motivation behind the political chicanery informing the decision, the outcome of it spoke volumes for where Ali now stood. The people who ran boxing in Hawaii, a state that exists literally and metaphorically on the fringes of the American national imagination, were prepared to go to extraordinary lengths to avoid having to host an Ali fight. The prospect of being one of the cities that could be featured in the most storied résumé in the sport, alongside everywhere from Kuala Lumpur to Kinshasa, from Manila to Munich, was no longer alluring.

During their deliberations, the Hawaiians had also received a troubling cable from London urging them not to sanction an Ali fight. At its first meeting since the Gardner bout had been proposed, the British Boxing Board of Control (who held the Englishman's license), was adamant it did not want one of its fighters being the next man to face such a diminished version of Ali.

"The Board's position is clear with regard to Ali," said secretary Ray Clark. "We are strongly opposed to Ali continuing boxing. The chairman has stated this previously and the board endorsed this view today."

The more vehement the opposition became, the louder those around Ali began to shout.

"It's his fight," said Harold Smith. "If the fight is made it will take place in one of three places: Kingston, Jamaica; the Bahamas; or Puerto Rico. It definitely won't take place in the United States, mainly because the media in the United States would be too hard on Ali."

That much was certainly true, because some in the press were already having fun at his expense.

"Muhammad Ali has arranged to fight John L Gardner," wrote legendary columnist Red Smith in the *New York Times*, "if they can find a place where the cops will look the other way."

Ali turned thirty-nine on January 17, 1981, and many papers across America that morning carried an interview that the Associated Press had conducted with him the previous day. Befitting somebody starting to realize that so many in boxing no longer wished to see him fight, or, indeed, would allow him to do so on their patches, his mood was fiery.

"I'm at war with the factors in boxing that want me to quit. I'm fighting them. I'm going to show them I'm too big for them. I'm not just an ordinary Christian American Negro. I'm a world-accepted Muslim. I'm doing this just for spite, to show them I'm too big to stop."

Claiming that he'd been contacted by five different countries (Japan was rumored to be in the mix) offering to host the fight, he refused to name them for fear of jeopardizing negotiations. Sounding predictably upbeat about his chances of beating Holmes in a rematch somewhere down the line, he also mused about aging and the fight game.

"The reason that I'm doing this is that I don't want nobody telling me what I can do or can't do as far as my occupation is concerned. I might say forget it even before I fight Holmes again. I just want the right to do what I want to do if I want to. A lot of fighters get knocked cold several times and keep on fighting, heavyweights in my division, and they haven't stopped them. If the authorities won't accept me, I'll go to the authorities of other worlds."

By which he probably meant Puerto Rico. He had previous experience there.

When he fought Jean-Pierre Coopman, the so-called Lion of Flanders, in San Juan in 1976, he was still near his box office peak. Six hundred fans paid $5 each day just to see him train. While the Roberto Clemente Coliseum only held 10,000, another 11,000 Puerto Ricans crowded into a stadium next door to watch a live television feed of him dismantling the overmatched Belgian, finally ending the contest in the fifth round.

But that was five years before. An eternity in boxing. An age in promotional terms, too. Although Ali applied for a license in Puerto Rico and the talk was of an April fight at the Hiram Bithorn Stadium, a baseball diamond, doubts now existed about whether San Juan was that interested. Of course, through all the embarrassing refusals, Gardner remained willing to go wherever was needed for the fight to happen. Well, sort of. He, too, had some reservations.

"As a fan, I think Ali should not box again and not get a license," said Gardner. "As a professional boxer, I hope he gets his license. This fight could set me up financially for life. If I beat him many would say Ali was an old man and over the hill. But it would still go into the record books, and I would be the only British boxer who had ever beaten the great Muhammad Ali. That is what would matter to me."

That and the proposed purse of $300,000 (it had shrunk from initial suggestions of half a million), which would make it the biggest payday of Gardner's life. His had been a plodding career, and he'd only become European champion after the title was taken off Italy's Lorenzo Zeno, who took a lucrative world title shot against Larry Holmes rather than defend the belt.

"If I personally had my way, Ali would not fight again, but I'm saying that as an Ali fan," said Mickey Duff, adding his voice to those questioning the moral if not financial wisdom of the whole enterprise. "As Gardner's manager, I have a responsibility to my fighter. Still, if I thought that by saying 'no' that would cause Ali's retirement, I would recommend to Gardner that he not fight Ali. But there are at least two opponents waiting in the wings if Gardner says no, and I think he's as eligible as anyone else to fight Ali and this might be the fight to convince him to retire before he does get hurt."

Hawaii and Puerto Rico soon faded from the conversation, and rumors began that Ali had turned his sights on Africa as a potential location. There were reports out of Morocco that he now wished for his "last" fight to take place in an Islamic state, and that Casablanca was the leading contender. Nothing would come of that either.

If January had proved a month when doors were closed in his face all over the planet, there was, amid the steady drip of negative headlines and steadfast refusals, one cameo that reminded everybody what all the fuss was about, why Ali was such a big deal.

Shortly after 2:00 p.m. on Monday, January 19, Joseph Brisbon began to climb the fire escape of a high-rise building on Wilshire Boulevard in Los Angeles. Upon reaching the ninth floor, the twenty-one-year-old eased himself out onto the ledge and shouted that he intended to commit suicide. The police were quickly called to the scene and, as this African-American man in a hooded sweatshirt and jeans started to roar in military jargon about the Viet Cong coming to get him, the commotion drew a crowd onto the street below.

The first cops to answer the 911 call tried their best to reason with Brisbon, but soon realized more serious professional help was needed. A psychologist was brought up to the ninth floor to try to persuade him to move back to safety and to reconsider. To no avail. A police chaplain spoke to him at length but, again, there was no convincing the poor man that ending his life was not the best option. Brisbon remained balancing precariously on the ledge for so long that some onlookers on the sidewalk below could be heard laughing and joking about his plight, intermittently shouting up at him, "Jump! Jump!"

This was the scene when Howard Bingham, photographer and Muhammad Ali's best friend, happened to come upon the crowd. He watched the drama play out for a bit, then approached a police officer and offered to call Ali (who lived nearby) to get him to come over to try to coax this distraught character in from the edge. Bingham had traveled the world with the boxer and witnessed his extraordinary impact on men, women, and children of every creed in every situation. Surely, it was worth a shot. The officer in charge thought not but, undeterred, Bingham took matters into his own hands.

"I went back to my car and called Ali anyway," he said. "I told Ali there was a guy up here on a building about a mile from his house, and maybe he could get through."

Minutes later, Ali's Rolls-Royce came driving the wrong way up Wilshire, lights flashing, and his horn occasionally beeping people out of the way. Initially, the officers busily trying to prevent a man plummeting to the pavement were not thrilled by the fighter's arrival. In the home of Hollywood, the last thing they wanted was to encourage celebrity involvement in trying to save potential suicides. Unsurprisingly, their first move was to refuse to allow Ali into the building. Then matters on high took a turn for the worse.

"He [Brisbon] said he was definitely going to jump, and actually came close to jumping," said Sergeant Bruce Hagerty. "We decided to give Muhammad a chance at talking to the man."

Once he reached the ninth floor, Ali opened a window just yards from where Brisbon was perched and stuck his head out.

"It's really you!" shouted Brisbon.

It was really him, immaculately turned out in a suit and tie. Now those gathered below were treated to the sight of the most famous athlete on the planet chatting with a man struggling to find a reason to live. Even by the bizarre standards of tall tales in Tinseltown, this was turning into quite an epic drama.

Then, Ali did what Ali had always done best. He instantly connected with somebody in that wonderful way he had about him. He learned quickly that Brisbon was depressed because he couldn't find a job and had issues with his parents. After chatting from the nearby window, Ali asked if he could move to the stairwell of the fire escape to make it a little easier to talk. For the first time all day, Brisbon agreed to allow someone into his immediate vicinity.

"The police thought he had a gun," said Ali. "Nobody would go near him. I told him I'm coming out and don't shoot me. He said, 'I won't shoot you, I don't even have a gun.' I took his word and walked on out."

The conversation continued with Ali now standing in the fire escape almost close enough to touch Brisbon, who remained, in every way, on the edge.

"I'm no good," said Brisbon. "I'm no good."

"You're my brother," said Ali. "I love you and I wouldn't lie to you. You got to listen. I want you to come home with me, meet some friends of mine."

"Why do you worry about me?" asked Brisbon. "I'm a nobody."

"You ain't a nobody!" said Ali, so moved by the plight of the young man that he started to cry.

"He saw me weeping and he couldn't believe I was really doing that, that I cared that much about him."

Ali assured Brisbon he'd help him find a job and he'd even intercede with his parents on his behalf. But, he also warned him that the step he was trying to take had a finality to it.

"If you jump," he warned his new friend, "you're going to hell because there's no way to repent."

More than once during an encounter that lasted twenty minutes, journalists watching from below were certain that Brisbon was going to go through with his desperate threat. Finally, he clambered back in off the ledge and fell sobbing into the embrace of Ali, the moment captured by the television cameras which, by then, were inevitably in attendance. The pair of them walked back into the building.

As a testament to the powers of Ali, it was a magnificent moment. When all else failed, he leapt into action and saved the day, leading even the staid CBS Evening News to compare him to a "superhero." Larry Holmes might have exposed the stark nature of his physical decline in Vegas three months earlier, but here was evidence that the charisma, the personality, and the magnetism remained undiminished.

It's not so much that no other athlete could have pulled it off; it's that no other athlete would probably even have tried. Supremely confident in his own ability, Ali didn't seem to give the awful possibility of failure a second thought as he stayed the course with Brisbon. He followed through on a promise made during the negotiation that he would ferry him to the Veterans' Hospital for a psychiatric evaluation, and spent $1,800 of his money paying for new clothes and an apartment for him.

As they left the building together, strolling towards the Rolls-Royce, the remaining onlookers chanted "USA! USA!" in a bizarre endpoint to the episode.

"He knows my address," said Ali later. "I've told people to bring him to me when they let him go. I'll help him. He knows he's got a home, my home."

Among the entourage accompanying Ali into and out of the building that day was Norman Thrasher, a member of the famous Detroit R&B group, The Midnighters. Now known as Norman Bilal Muhammad, Thrasher had embraced the Nation of Islam in the late 1950s and was an old friend of Ali's. The pair first met when they attended the same mosque in Miami in the early 1960s.

If Thrasher was a familiar presence in the ever-changing crowd that always seemed to orbit Ali, there was a less well-known figure also along for the ride on Wilshire Boulevard. That was James Cornelius, a friend of a more recent vintage who was blown away by what he'd just witnessed.

"Even now I am still awed by how Ali was able to quickly and effectively gain the confidence of that young man," wrote Cornelius. "I had read stories and I had seen pictures of people being coaxed not to take their own lives, but even in the movies the task is wrenching and time-consuming. But for the Champ, plucking Joe back to reality seemed effortless. He approached the task with the same air and confidence with which he faced his opponents in the ring."

And, it turned out, Cornelius was determined to be the man to help Ali get back into that ring.

CHAPTER TWO
The Sweet Science of Fraud

This will be my last fight. It's got to the point where it's not the money. It's your name. It's hearing the people when you're on top that's important. I just want to get my title back, then preach my religion.
Muhammad Ali, Deer Lake, PA, August 26, 1974

JAMES CORNELIUS WAS A STUDENT at Henry McNeal Turner High School in Atlanta when he first heard the name Cassius Clay. He was working part-time as a bus boy at the Riviera Motel on Peachtree Street one day in 1964 when he saw all his co-workers poring over a newspaper. They were drinking in reports of how Clay had downed Sonny Liston and become champion of the world. A story to fire any teen imagination.

More than a decade later, Cornelius finally got to shake the hand of the man who ended Liston's reign. By then Clay had morphed into Muhammad Ali, and the teenager had also changed his name and embraced Islam. As a member of Atlanta's Temple #15, home base of the Reverend Elijah Muhammad (leader of the Nation of Islam), he now went by James X Cornelius, and many in the Muslim community bought cars from him at his used car lot in the south-west of the city.

Cornelius also supplied surplus U.S. Mail vehicles to the Fruit of Islam, the paramilitary wing of the Nation, which was running a very successful fish distribution program in the Georgian capital and other cities across America. When he was introduced to Ali in the late 1970s, Cornelius was known around town as "auto man," and had the reputation of somebody always helpful to a co-religionist needing a set of wheels.

However, the nickname and the popularity disguised the fact that he was not quite the businessman he made himself out to be. In 1975, he pled guilty to five counts of theft, agreed to pay $23,000 back to individuals and banks, and was placed on five years' probation. By 1980, there was also an ongoing investigation into his dealings with Trust Company Bank and several other financial institutions around Georgia. In particular, the FBI were chasing down a link between him and a bank official with whom he did regular business.

Not for the first time, a criminal past was no barrier to gaining Ali's confidence. Somehow, Cornelius used his Nation of Islam connections to inveigle his way into the fighter's inner circle during the buildup to the Larry Holmes bout. Indeed, that evening in Las Vegas he was part of the entourage in the dressing room, and even walked to the ring with Ali. Not long afterwards, by then down on his luck financially, Cornelius decided it was time to cash in on the relationship.

Originally, Cornelius had a plan to run a golf tournament with Ali's name attached to it. He'd even contacted the LPGA Tour with an eye on meeting to discuss it further. It all seemed very plausible and possible, except for one problem: the small matter of him being on the FBI's radar and the subject of an ongoing investigation. To try to escape scrutiny, Cornelius secured a new identity from a contact in law enforcement in Georgia. Replete with a state-issued driver's license and a fresh Social Security number, he relocated from Atlanta to California. The mountain would move to Muhammad.

"By Christmas Eve 1980 I had packed all my clothes, put my wife and sons in the car, and struck out for Los Angeles where we found a nice secluded hotel," wrote Cornelius in his memoir. "We stayed there for eleven days until we found a house to lease. My personal problems with drugs mounted, but somehow things moved along. We had looked at several houses for rent or lease, and finally set our sights on one at 616 South Arden Boulevard, only seconds from where Ali lived."

A man battling addiction, struggling to get by financially, opted to live in an impressive property worth $600,000. Brazen and audacious, and perhaps the first sign that all was not as it seemed to be. The rent may have been steep, but the proximity to Ali ensured Cornelius quickly became a fixture in the scene around the fighter in the first half of 1981—witness his box seat to the suicide episode on Wilshire Boulevard.

This then would be the man to pull together the disparate threads and organize Ali's final fight. How could that happen? Why? Well, Howard Bingham had one theory to explain the way so many charlatans managed to penetrate the inner sanctum.

"All someone had to do was walk in the door and say 'As-salaam-alaikum'," said Bingham. "That was the easiest way to plug him."

In his own recollection of that time, Cornelius claims that one day early in 1981, as the pair of them were watching television at Ali's mansion in Hancock Park, the fighter turned to him and said, "I want to rumble," a statement that inspired his fellow Muslim to do everything in his power to facilitate Ali's return to the ring. Of course, this version of events ignores the fact that Ali had been busy trying to be allowed to rumble for months by that point.

Cornelius was striking up a relationship at a very curious time in Ali's career. Not only did the big promoters no longer want any part of him now that he was a spent force, his name had also been tarnished by association with a shyster named Harold Smith. A sports promoter who'd met Ali through his involvement with the one-time American sprinting prospect Houston McTear, Smith had decided to try his hand at boxing, using the name of the biggest fighter of all to open doors.

Smith paid Ali for the right to call his company Muhammad Ali Professional Sports (MAPS), and that was enough cachet to get him taken seriously in most gyms. It helped, too, that his reputation in that world was quickly enhanced by lavish spending and a penchant for always carrying a briefcase full of cash, the kind of eye-catching accoutrement that can impress fighters or their managements to put their names on contracts.

"I saw him with all those beautiful girls, planes, boats," said Ali when it became apparent Smith had been involved in defrauding the Beverly Hills branch of Wells Fargo Bank for $21.3 million. "I used to say, 'You sure everything's okay, Harold?' He always said everything was fine. I still don't know where he gets his money. I'm still wondering."

The way in which Smith offered outrageous purses made many suspect he was too good to be true. There was lurid speculation his largesse was being underwritten by the mob and/or drug dealers. The truth was much less glamorous. He was just ripping off a bank with the help of a couple of people on the inside.

At the time that the FBI began snooping around MAPS, Smith was putting together a spectacular night of boxing at Madison Square Garden for February 23, 1981. Headlined by a Ken Norton versus Gerry Cooney bout, there was going to be $8 million in guaranteed purses and three world title fights on the card. Smith was also trying to interest networks in a television show featuring MAPS ring card girls called *Ali's Angels*.

Although Ali had no part in, or knowledge of, the fraud or Smith's ambitions to branch into Hollywood, the presence of his name alone ensured that the scandal became big news. He was at a benefit night at the Grand Hyatt Hotel in New York when the MAPS story finally broke. Cheerleaders greeted him when he exited the elevator, chanting his name, even as reporters scurried around him asking questions about Smith and the disappearing money.

"I always find a way to stay in the news, don't I?" Ali whispered to one journalist, and to some veteran writers he appeared almost invigorated by the attention, relishing, whatever the circumstances, the presence of cameras back in his face.

"Do you have $8 million to save the promotion?" shouted one reporter.

"I got $8 million easy," said Ali.

With comments like that, there was immediate pressure on him to step in and underwrite the event at the Garden, which was then three weeks away. He very quickly and smartly rowed back from his original assertion about having enough money to save the day.

"Harold Smith was stealing money," said Ali. "We can't pay those prices. No promoter can. The fighters and the managers have to agree to other terms. The card as originally presented was unreasonable from the start. Now when we read the papers we know where he got those unrealistic figures from."

Yet, he couldn't help talking up his ability to maybe segue into promotion.

"I made Don King," said Ali. "I made Bob Arum. I am the greatest name in boxing and I will be the greatest promoter. Everyone will come to me. I will use my name to run things. People shouldn't condemn boxing. Because Nixon was no good doesn't mean the government was bad."

When he returned to Los Angeles from New York, Ali was confronted by a phalanx of reporters staking out his home in case Smith, who'd become a fugitive at that point, might turn up there. Again, his responses to questions had him speaking out of both sides of his mouth.

One minute sensible….

"I decided to take my name off the organization a few days before it happened because it just didn't look right. Whoever knew it was going to break told my lawyer."

The next almost bragging about his unwitting role in the fraud…

"I am always wrapped in controversy. Controversy is my middle name. Ain't many names that can steal this much."

Asked how he might react if Smith visited him, he said, "I'm going to tell him go right to the FBI before he talks to me. I'm not going to jail. I'm going to tell Harold, 'Turn yourself in, don't talk to me.'"

Did he know where Harold was?

"Where's Harold? It would be illegal for me to know where Harold is and not tell anybody."

Amid all the controversy, it emerged that Smith (whose real name it turns out was Ross Eugene Fields) had been trying to add Ali-Gardner to the promotion at Madison Square Garden, telling the people in New York he wanted to do so as a favor to Ali. As the questions kept coming, it also sounded as though Ali might finally be seeing sense about the possibility of one more bout.

"Another fight was just something I had in myself…to come back," he said during one bout of MAPS-related questioning by journalists. "All I'm going to do now is promote and lecture. I ain't fighting. I don't need fighting. I'm going to stay out of the ring but I haven't retired."

In the spring of 1981, Ali was somewhere he'd never been before. Still smarting from the beatdown he'd received at the hands of his former sparring partner in Vegas, he'd become a bit-part player in a case of fraud that was, to that point, the biggest bank scandal in American history. Much as he tried to brazen out the MAPS stuff, even turning up to support Smith in court during closing arguments before he was sentenced to ten years in prison, the constant drip of negative headlines must have hurt.

For the ego, this was probably difficult to take, and certainly wasn't what he envisaged for his post-career life. Against that background, it seems obvious he would inevitably return to the prospect of one more fight, and would be amenable to anybody promising to make that happen. The ring offered salvation, the chance to rid himself of the sour taste of the Holmes defeat, the toxic fall-out from the MAPS debacle, and provide the opportunity to turn the clock back with one more win that would generate the positive coverage he thrived on.

All of this explains why James Cornelius could, at that time, have Ali's ear and style himself as the man to pave the way for his return to the ring and the spotlight he so desperately coveted. Just how somebody with no money, no track record in promotion, and no contacts in the sport beyond a friendship with one fighter, could pull off such a feat is a remarkable tale, an amalgam of derring-do, brinksmanship, and barefaced lying.

It was Harold Smith who'd first proposed the Bahamas as a possible location for Ali's sixty-first fight, and once Cornelius decided to focus his efforts on securing the bout he set his sights on the Caribbean island. Not yet a decade free of colonial rule from London, the newly-independent nation seemed a perfect fit, a country that would relish the opportunity of the international publicity that traditionally came with hosting an Ali fight, even with him now in the post-twilight of his career.

Undoubtedly, that's how Cornelius sold it to the Bahamian officials and politicians he met on two trips to Nassau in the spring and summer of 1981. Deal-making skills honed in the secondhand car business in Atlanta stood him in good stead as he navigated the island's labyrinthine corridors of power. An initial contact with Cyril Ijeoma at the accounting firm of Laventhol and Horwarth gained him an introduction to Kendal W. Nottage, the Minister of Youth, Sports and Cultural Affairs.

A curious character with a résumé that included banning reggae music from the nation's radios, and a stint working as Howard Hughes's lawyer, Nottage had the ear of Lynden O. Pindling, the Prime Minister, and he had the ability to make things happen. Whatever his motivation, he bought into what Cornelius was selling, endorsing the fight and guaranteeing that Ali would be licensed to box.

If that was something for the would-be promoter to work with, pulling off any sort of bout in Nassau still appeared an awfully big ask. Having a location and the tacit approval of the star attraction represented progress, but there was a long way to go. A penniless man living under an assumed name is always going to struggle to raise the high finance necessary to underwrite an Ali promotion.

That much was hammered home during Cornelius's second trip to Nassau. He arrived at LAX with ten dollars in his pocket, bought a plane ticket with a check that was destined to bounce while he was in the air, and then went cap in hand to the Bahamians who'd been so helpful during his first visit. Whatever he lacked in organizational skills, Cornelius was an audacious character and something of a master at flying by the seat of his pants.

For much of the time when he was trying to pull together the proposed fight in Nassau, his office was the payphone of a Shoney's Restaurant. It was noisy and far from ideal, but his home phone had been disconnected, so he needed some place from where to call prospective investors. Given that kind of chaos, Ali and Herbert Muhammad appeared to question the validity of his enterprise at different stages. Indeed, at a certain point Cornelius shamelessly played the religion card, reminding Ali of all the work he'd done for the Nation in Atlanta in the seventies. And there was no doubt in his own mind that a higher power was guiding his promotion.

"Muhammad Ali said to me, 'I want to fight again,'" said Cornelius. "I knew that the help he needed from me would be difficult, but by Allah's permission, the designer and planner of all things, it happened."

That Ali himself was in two minds about his future was clear from a trip to Portland, Oregon, in the middle of June 1981. Following a visit to The Oregon Freeze Dry Foods plant in Albany, where he discussed an initiative to use the company's products to help feed the hungry in Third World countries, he caused a huge stir at the local airport upon his departure. When questioned about his professional intentions, he was, at first, unequivocal.

"I don't have nothing to do with boxing. I've been blessed to be bigger than boxing. Boxing was just a medium to get me in the position I'm in now. My work is only beginning."

About half an hour later, by which time he had been besieged by well-wishers and adoring fans, he changed his tune.

"Just one more fight—maybe?"

For all Ali's public ambivalence, as the summer wore on Cornelius appeared to have the outline of an arrangement for a December bout in Nassau. Until, all of a sudden, he didn't.

On Wednesday, August 19, Ali flew to Columbia, South Carolina, and, in the now familiar fashion, announced before he'd left the airport that he was there to show that a man nearing forty could still fight. Ahead of a tentative bout against an unnamed opponent set for November 1, he was in town to take a complete physical in order to gain a license to box.

"It's risky," he said. "But life is risky. It's attitude that causes success or failure."

Conveniently ignoring the Bahamas, he listed Libya, Egypt, and Morocco as countries that desperately wanted to stage the bout. And, ever the name-dropper, pointed out that Leonid Brezhnev and Deng Xiaoping ("I know him personally") had assured him that he could always fight in the USSR or China. There may even have been some truth to those boasts, but the philanthropist in him was offering a city in the south a chance to gain worldwide recognition.

"The whole world's gonna come to Columbia, South Carolina. Columbia, South Carolina will be known in Morocco. This shall be the greatest event of all time. Of all time! My man! My comeback!"

And, of course, amid the bluster he claimed that his mission had a higher purpose than just boxing.

"I'm actually teaching the world, teaching the deprived people, teaching the minority people, people who give up. I'm back and I want to be an inspiration to everybody not to quit. All of you have a Larry Holmes in your life."

On the Wednesday night, Ali turned up at the Memorial Youth Center in Columbia. A reporter covering his visit reckoned he looked tired as he moved through the crowd, stopping to kiss babies and to sign autographs, his progress that of a politician courting voters. Yet, when he was challenged to climb into the ring by a couple of local contenders he was a man transformed. Newly invigorated, unbuttoning a black shirt that covered a midriff that was paunchier than he'd have liked, he started mouthing off at a succession of would-be contenders.

"I got speed, I got endurance, if you gonna fight me, you're gonna need more insurance!"

Sylvester "KO" Conners, a Golden Gloves champion, was first up, gleefully taking the bait and starting to jaw back. Never a good move. Ali accused him of talking too much and then during a brief spar he began evading and swatting away the youngster's attempted punches. "Man, you're so ugly when you start crying the tears go halfway down your face and then turn around and come back."

Roger Kirkpatrick was next to try his luck, and he came with something of a pedigree. Last time Ali had swept through town, he'd got to spar with him then, too. That was ten years earlier.

On this particular night, Kirkpatrick assured Ali, "I'm going to get you in shape for Larry Holmes!" Ali slipped most of Kirkpatrick's punches and only threw a few brief flurries himself. When he landed with one, however, he mock-chanted "Larry Holmes, Larry Holmes!" to the delight of those necklacing the ring. As Kirkpatrick climbed through the ropes, he pointed to the spot on his face where one of Ali's jabs had connected, and said, "I'm not gonna wash my face for a week."

The following morning, there was a news conference at the Carolina Coliseum that featured a coup de theatre for the gathered reporters. Ali opened his wallet, took out a crisp five dollar bill and handed it to Chris Hitopoulos, Richland County's boxing commissioner. Hitopoulos then presented him with a license to fight.

"This is the place where they let me make my comeback," said Ali. "I couldn't get a license to box from the good white folks in the liberal North. That shows how hypocritical all those Northern cities are."

As if to hammer home the legitimacy of the enterprise, a team of four doctors were present, the same physicians who it was reported had put him through four hours of rigorous testing the day before. They pronounced Ali in "good shape."

"All of us agree he's in perfect health excepting the stress cardiogram which would be perfect when he gets back to full training," said Dr. Christopher Biser. "He was at about eighty-eight percent. That's excellent considering he's not in full training. We expected his weight to be a little more than his fighting weight, but it's not as bad as in the past."

Biser recommended that Ali plane twenty pounds off his bulging frame of 244 by the day of the fight. At one point, somebody mentioned that Joe Frazier was also planning a comeback. Ali was dismissive. "He's too old!" Of course, Frazier was two years younger than Ali, but he never did let the facts get in the way of a good quip. In any case he was supremely confident there'd be no shortage of fighters willing to take him on.

"We'll get offers," said Ali. "They'll knock the doors down. Whoever fights me will be honored. We will choose one of them if they are lucky, that's my attitude. I'm still pretty. Look at me. A little heavy. I'll lose some weight, get in shape, make my comeback. I will train one month here in Columbia so people can see me in living color."

Ali was so sanguine about the whole thing that he began mapping out his schedule for the next year, plotting to fight the number eight contender and then the number four contender before demanding a world title shot. And, in his opinion, by that point Gerry Cooney, the Long Islander, should have dethroned Larry Holmes, setting up a clash between the latest great white hope and "the greatest." That would be box office gold for all involved.

"Me and Cooney? For $20 million a piece, a $40 million gate. The Ku Klux Klan will be selling tickets and all the bigots will rant and rave, 'Stop the nigger! Stop the nigger!' Whoever can put the behinds on seats has the power. I can still put behinds in the seats."

The trip to South Carolina seemed like a success—except nothing was to come of it. For all the headlines and the glad-handing and the very public handover of the license, Columbia was very quickly put in the rearview mirror. Just ten days after the southern swing, James Cornelius called a press conference for September 1 at New York's Waldorf-Astoria Hotel to announce Ali's comeback fight. Even if he had been charging telegrams to somebody else's account in order to finalize the details, Cornelius had at least enough in place to make an announcement.

Aside from its location in the media capital of the world, the venue for the press conference was chosen because this was a place with which the fighter had a unique and storied history.

The first time Ali had checked into the Waldorf he was eighteen-year-old Cassius Clay. It was September 1960, and he'd just gotten off a plane from the Rome Olympics as the freshly-minted light-heavyweight champion. Wearing his gold medal around his neck and still clad in the official Team USA jacket, he stayed in a suite, and once put away five steaks in a single day. The luxury accommodation and the overeating was underwritten by Billy Reynolds, an aluminum mogul from Louisville desperate to secure Clay's signature on his first professional contract.

Fourteen years later, the institution on Park Avenue played host to an event designed to promote the forthcoming "Rumble in the Jungle" against George Foreman. With the eyes of the world upon him that day, it is most often remembered as the occasion when he delivered a soliloquy destined to be filed in the annals of sports history under the simple, self-explanatory headline, "How Great I Am!"

"I done rassled with an alligator, I done tousled with a whale, I done handcuffed lightning, threw thunder in jail," rapped Ali. "That's bad. Only last week, I murdered a rock, hospitalized a brick. I'm so mean I make medicine sick. Bad...fast. Last night I cut the light off my bedroom, hit the switch and was in the bed before the room was dark. You, George Foreman, all you chumps are gonna bow when I whoop'em, all of you. I know you got 'im picked but the man's in trouble. Imma show you how great I am..."

At that point in 1974, Ali was the most famous athlete in the world, the most loquacious in front of a microphone and, very often, the only show in every town he ever visited. Now, on this day in 1981, he was back in the same hotel, in the very same ballroom with the distinctive high ceilings. The setting was familiar. The purpose of the visit was, much as before, to sell an upcoming fight. But it was different this time. Oh so very different.

When Ali took his seat at the dais he was wearing a gray suit, blue shirt and tie, and was carrying a briefcase. For all the world, he looked like a middle-aged businessman about to deliver a keynote speech to a company conference. He even went through the motions of taking a sheaf of papers from the case and shuffling them on the table in front of him.

"When did Ali ever need a script?" whispered one reporter.

The emcee for the occasion was Philip Davis. Introducing himself as the general counsel for Sports Internationale Bahamas, a promotional outfit that Cornelius had hastily put together in the previous weeks, he formally announced that Ali's next fight would take place at the Queen Elizabeth Sports Center, a baseball field, in Nassau. Despite having no fixed date for the contest, Davis claimed to be in negotiations with some of the top heavyweight contenders for what he grandiloquently described as "the greatest comeback in the history of boxing."

It says much for the chaotic nature of the presentation that a provisional date (December 2) and an opponent (Trevor Berbick) would both be revealed by Ali before the press conference was finished.

"Ladies and gentlemen, this is a historic moment for the Bahamas," said Davis, giving it the hard sell. "And having spoken to Mr. Muhammad Ali, an historic moment in his life, in his comeback trail towards being the champion of the world."

Perhaps conscious of so many events in his life and career that were genuinely historic, Ali chose not to situate the bout in such bombastic terms. No doubt keenly aware of the public's lack of appetite to see him fight again, he preferred to offer justification for his decision.

"Everybody questions why I want to do this," said Ali. "Why? Because it's there. It's something I've got to do. Why did we go to the moon? Because it's there. They say, 'You've won it three times, be satisfied with that.' But we weren't satisfied with the moon. Now we're going to Mars and Venus and Saturn because they're there. No one has ever won the heavyweight championship four times. I must be the first man to do it."

If the familiar face delivering these lines was thicker than ever before, the scrum of writers and photographers detailed to capture his latest utterances was decidedly thinner than it used to be. The most generous count estimated two dozen microphones perched in front of him. What would have been a huge press turnout for any other public figure was, by Ali's own lofty standards, an indicator of his falling stock. Even for newspaper editors, he was no longer as magnetic a draw as he once had been.

"I won't let you tell me I'm through," he continued. "I've never been a quitter. I've always liked challenges. Do I look like an old man to you with gray hair? People give up too easy. They quit too easy. I love challenges. I must pursue my aspirations and dreams. Don't tell me it can't be done. I'm out to prove it can be."

He was doing his best to provide a convincing narrative: aggrieved fighter seeks one more chance to defeat Father Time. But having announced his last retirement in 1979, this was his second comeback in less than two years and every media report of the event described him as "subdued," perhaps the word least associated with him over the previous two decades in the public glare. On this occasion, though, it was the correct adjective.

"He stood on the dais, all polished and spruced up like an antique car, the relic he is," wrote Will Grimsley, who'd been covering Ali for the AP since the early 1960s. "Kick his tires and the wheels shimmy. Raise the hood and the engine is a mess of pipes and tubes, bent and rusty. Turn the key and you get a labored chug. That's Muhammad Ali, vintage 1960s in the year 1981."

The passion and bravura of before were just not there. The carnival barker cum rapper who had taunted Foreman with such verbal dexterity and humor in this same room just seven years earlier seemed a very distant memory. This was a decaffeinated Ali. The voice was the same. The delivery remained almost note perfect. But there was just something missing.

This was Ali at the most awkward stage any public figure can reach, the moment it becomes apparent he has stayed on too long. This was Elvis Presley in Vegas, still demanding the spotlight, still belting out the beloved hits, yet so obviously a star of lesser wattage than he used to be. This was Willie Mays stumbling around the New York Mets' outfield trying to chase down treacherous balls that used to so easily die in his glove.

Even when he called out the *New York Daily News* cartoonist Bill Gallo for depicting him as a geriatric, there was no zing to Ali's lines.

"I see cartoons in the paper—Gallo!" said Ali. "Do I look like an old man to you? Got a couple of little grays but basically I'm still nice-lookin' man. You [the press] all say I looked so bad in my last fight. What if I threw up my arms and said, 'I quit,' and walked out?"

It was no coincidence that he would invoke Roberto Duran saying "No mas," and calling a halt to his welterweight title bout against Sugar Ray Leonard the previous November. Those around Ali knew that he was very envious of how Leonard, Duran, Marvin Hagler, and Thomas Hearns had captured the public imagination now, becoming the faces of the sport like he once had been, and doing so while drawing down astronomical purses for their contests.

"I've shocked the world ever since the Sonny Liston fight," said Ali. "Now twenty-one years later, I continue to shock the world."

That it was actually only seventeen years since he fought Liston was a telling and slightly troubling detail. Still, he pressed on with his attempt to convince the doubters.

"Look at how I'm sweating," he said, as he mopped his brow with a blue handkerchief. "When I lost to Larry Holmes in Las Vegas, I wasn't sweating at all. Imagine it—114 degrees—and I'm not even sweating. Something was terribly wrong with me. I'm 240 pounds now and I can do better at this moment than I did that night."

That theme was taken up, unprompted, by a voice from the back of the room. "The champ was sick that night in Vegas!" roared Bundini Brown, Ali's legendary cornerman, wearing a button emblazoned with the slogan he'd coined all those years ago, "Float like a butterfly, Sting like a bee." If that quote was, like much else in the room, a reminder of how things were in the glory days, Brown gave value for money once the spotlight reached him.

"This is the year of the handicapped," shouted Brown. "The blind and the crippled climbed a mountain where people who could see and hear failed. A 135-year-old lady in Russia went to her son's birthday party. A Canadian with a peg leg runs clear across the country—2,000 miles—to raise money for cancer. The mind controls the body. You gotta have faith. Against Holmes, the champ lost too much weight, tried to be pretty before he was strong. He brought beauty in and left the beast out. He brought in the butterfly and forgot the bee. It will be different this time."

When one reporter asked how much Ali was getting for the fight, his attorney Michael Phenner leaned over and responded, "That's between Mr. Ali and the Internal Revenue Service." Later, the press was briefed that his purse would be "in the millions." That might have been the hope, but as soon as it emerged that Canada's hardly box-office Berbick, who'd recently gone the distance in losing to Holmes, was the opponent, everybody in the fight game knew that number was an aspiration rather than a genuinely attainable goal.

"He who is not courageous enough to take a risk in life will accomplish nothing," said Ali, finally offering a quote with a little bit of depth to go with all the ersatz braggadocio. Or maybe not.

"Ali was once again basking in the sunlight and enjoying every second," wrote James Cornelius. "But underneath this façade, I could somehow sense some real trepidation and even a tinge of sadness in the Champ's voice. To me, he seemed to be trying to convince himself he could make this comeback, but he was deep down unsure of his abilities."

Cornelius was in a unique position to know Ali's mood and to read the signs, having spent so much time in his orbit during his own quixotic quest over the previous nine months. Of course, it was telling that Cornelius wasn't mentioned in the Waldorf-Astoria that day, or in the next morning's papers. The promoter cut a shadowy figure in the background. Very few knew who he was, where he came from, or what he was about. Well, nobody except the FBI, which had an open warrant out for his arrest, and whose file on his nefarious business activities was lengthy and growing.

In the meantime, attention turned to Ali's opponent, Trevor Berbick.

CHAPTER THREE
The Boy Who Learned to Fight at Gitmo

Horses get old, cars get old, the pyramids of Egypt are crumbling. I want to retire while I'm still on top. As of now, this is the last time you will see Muhammad Ali in a fight.

Muhammad Ali, Kuala Lumpur, June 1975

IN 1964, THE UNITED STATES began to phase out the Cuban civilians employed on the military base at Guantanamo Bay. Their replacements were guest workers from newly-independent Jamaica whose government assured Washington they'd supply and vet all the newcomers. Within three years, the Jamaican contingent numbered over 1,200, many of them underpaid and shoehorned into substandard, undersized Quonset huts in what was a rather convenient and cheap arrangement that simultaneously assuaged US Navy concerns about security and saved it millions of dollars.

In one telling of the tale, Trevor Berbick was coerced to move to Guantanamo as an eighteen-year-old by the Jamaican Department of Labor as part of a government training program. In another, he volunteered to go. Whatever the circumstances precipitating his arrival in the early 1970s, there's no doubt that, as formative experiences go, this one was life-changing. According to his own testimony, over the next five years he did stints as a receiving clerk, welder, salvage-diver, machine operator, and maître'd at the officers' mess. Somewhere along the way, he also learned to box.

"You've got to understand this," said Berbick. "This was during the Vietnam War and a lot of guys there were going wacko; some guys were waiting to be shipped off to war, others were coming back all busted up—legs gone, nerves shot. One time fifty ships were in the harbor and a lot of guys were all there for liberty. They'd drink and let off steam, and they'd fight anybody in the streets.

"They'd put a whuppin' on you if you couldn't handle yourself. One night a marine jumped me coming from work. But I learned a little martial arts from the Special Forces and handled him pretty well. He told me to come on down and join them boxing. I ended up beating the All-Marine heavyweight champ and winning the service tournament. After that I figured I had a shot at being a pretty good boxer."

In a later edition of the story, he claimed his fistic ambitions were actually born out of frustration at not being able to separate marines when they started brawling with each other in the mess, prompting him to take up the sport simply to make his day job of reluctant peace-maker a bit easier. However he was introduced to the ring, we know he found his way there, and inside the ropes he discovered something about himself. He could fight even if he had spent his whole life to that point believing he couldn't.

"I wasn't much of a fighter," said Berbick. "When I used to get hit at school I would cry, and my sister Beverly would have to take the other guy on. I had to prove later that I could take care of myself. I realized I didn't have what it takes."

In some interviews he gave, that story, too, was turned on its head, and he claimed that as a young kid he'd actually learned to fight so he could stand up to his older sibling, the fabled Beverly, who delivered a mean right hook and wasn't afraid to throw it in his direction.

Ordinarily, the fact that two competing narratives could exist about such a trivial aspect of his biography may not seem that important. Our memories of events can change over time. With Berbick, though, this is the rule, not the exception. There are several conflicting versions of so many major chapters in his life. Each one appears to contain a kernel of truth, the yarns just being spun in different directions at various points in his career, depending on the audience he was trying to impress.

"There are fragments of Trevor Berbick's story that can be told with conviction," wrote Chris Jones in 1999, "but there are holes in his life's narrative that even he is unable to fill."

This tendency perhaps contributed to the recurring confusion about his age. The official boxing records list August 1, 1954, as his date of birth. Yet, a random selection of clippings from all phases of his career show he's routinely listed as a year older or younger than that date indicates. Not to mention that those who first met him in Guantanamo were convinced, even back then, that he was at least five years older than he claimed to be.

"Legally," he once said, "I'm a spirit; I have no age."

If we don't know exactly when, we *can* say where. Berbick was, for certain, born in Port Antonio, a town in a stretch of Jamaica's northeast coast so idyllic it's beloved of Hollywood producers looking for blue skies, white sandy beaches, and a paradisiacal vibe. His father was an accountant with the National Banana Board and his mother ran a grocery store. The fourth of seven kids, his was a carefree childhood, full of clambering up coconut trees one minute, diving to set fish traps in the bay the next. This was not the typical boxer's tale of trying to fight his way out of the ghetto.

"I had nothing much to do except go to the beach and pick fruits," said Berbick in 1981. "If I had put my free time into something more constructive, I'd probably be farther along than I am now. I don't know what poverty is. I always had everything I wanted to eat and more."

Despite his parents harboring ambitions of him going to university, he had other ideas, making the short trip across the sea to Miami at seventeen in search of adventure. He spent a year working the cruise ships as a waiter, an occupation that alerted him to a wider world and to a whole range of different and difficult characters.

"The job wasn't bad and the tips were good," he said. "I learned to deal with people. I'm not just some dummy who knows only about fighting. I mean, I can understand the psychological. I know about life."

After the ersatz glamour of life on the oceangoing liners, he fetched up at Guantanamo where the Jamaican contingent worked out in a gym that reeked of sweat. When he finally started boxing there, the best equipment he had access to belonged to the American soldiers who'd buy it mail-order from the advertisements in *The Ring* magazine. One departing marine remembers going to collect his stuff and being beseeched by Berbick, "Mon, don't take the headgears." He left the gear behind because he felt bad about the primitive circumstances in which the Jamaicans were living.

"The marines are supposed to be tough," Berbick recalled. "They've got to believe that one marine should be able to beat up three ordinary guys. They feel they're superior. They'd go out on weekends and fight sailors, and that's how I'd get into hassles."

Whatever the exact circumstances of his ring debut, there's no question that in this small, insular community he instantly gained some renown as a fighter and an eccentric, the double-billing that he would carry with him for most of his sporting life. Aside from his toughness and strength, he became known for singing hymns at the top of his voice and ranting and raving about religion if the mood took him. He also developed a reputation as a man with a ferocious temper, best not to be crossed inside or outside the ring.

If that's how some of his contemporaries in Guantanamo recall him, one particular aspect of Berbick's own memory of the five years (sometimes he'd say it was four!) he spent at the Naval Station sounds a tad far-fetched. In an interview with the *Miami News* in 1986, he claimed that he also did some "secret work" for the United States government during his stint in its employ. Whatever the veracity of that outlandish boast, boxing definitely provided him with a route off the base.

Representing his home country, he took bronze at the 1975 Pan American Games in Mexico City, losing a semi-final decision to America's Michael Dokes, another fighter who'd go on to briefly hold a version of the world heavyweight title in the 1980s. The Jamaican Olympic trials the following year were an easier proposition. Berbick was the only contender in his division, often claiming the other heavyweights withdrew from the competition once they laid eyes on him. Either way, he earned a ticket to Montreal without throwing a punch, never having fought a single fight in his homeland, and all of this just a year after having his first serious amateur bout.

During the buildup to the Games, he spent part of his preparation in Halifax, Nova Scotia, working with Taylor Gordon, a trainer who put generations of Canadian Olympians through his hands. When Berbick was subsequently defeated by Romania's Mircea Simon, the eventual silver medalist, in his first bout of the tournament, he decided to stay on in the host nation, gradually migrating across to the only place in the country that he actually knew. In Halifax, the Gordons welcomed him with a warmth that stayed with him for a long time after.

"At the time he trained very hard; he was a very dedicated worker, a maniac in the gym," said Gordon. "His lifestyle at that time was good. We thought because the heavyweight class was always open to new faces and new ventures, we felt that he still had a chance of coming to the top."

He wasn't long for the amateur ranks. Soon, he had a manager in Don Kerr, a lawyer who had boxed in his youth, and a well-regarded local pro trainer in Tom McCluskey.

"When he came to me first, he was a stand-up, straight fighter," recalled McCluskey. "And he had no punch. For a heavyweight, he should've been able to hit harder, but he had his feet in the wrong position. So I got him settled down to where he had good balance and he could knock people out."

On September 27, 1976, he made his pro debut, stopping Wayne Martin (fighting for just the second and last time in his career) in the fifth of a scheduled six-rounder. Over the next three years he won ten in a row, nine inside the distance, at various venues in Nova Scotia. It was the kind of upward trajectory that gains a fighter followers. One

Canadian novelist remembers as a high school student being taken to see the rising star work out on the wrong side of town.

"Berbick's gym was in the North End, near an intersection whose very name, in my high school, was held to be scary," wrote Russell Smith. "It was near the naval base, near the housing project, in the shadow of the great suspension bridge across the harbour. We simply didn't go there, and because we didn't go there we imagined all kinds of terrors: We thought you'd get mugged, you'd get beaten, even in the daytime. We were proud even to be walking through the neighborhood. The gym was unheated. It was a sort of garage. There were plywood planks on the floor, a heavy bag and a speed bag, and a small raised ring."

There was enough equipment for Berbick to hone his craft and physique, and with each victory he gained there was inevitably talk of a showdown with George Chuvalo. Though he was then past forty, Chuvalo remained the biggest box office draw in the sport in the country, and there were several abortive attempts to get the pair to duel for the Canadian heavyweight title.

"I chased Chuvalo for a year and a half," said Berbick. "I used to have respect for the man. But how can he turn down $35,000 to come to Halifax when they wouldn't even guarantee me $5,000 to fight him in Toronto? Now he is telling all the heavyweights in Toronto not to fight me. What can I do?"

Berbick did go to extraordinary lengths to try to make the fight happen. On a visit to Halifax with his wife around this time, Chuvalo returned to his hotel room after dinner to find Berbick sitting there waiting. He was so desperate for an audience with the country's best-known heavyweight that he'd broken in.

"We walked in and there he was, large as life," recalled Chuvalo. "He kept smiling and saying he just wanted to meet me and be my friend, but I got mad and threw him out. Years later, when I got to know him a bit, he always struck me as being a bit wacky."

As 1978 drew to a close, Berbick was making a living as a fighter. Far from rich, he was nevertheless generous to those who'd helped him on his way. On Christmas Eve that year, a mysterious package was delivered to Taylor Gordon's house. When he opened the box, it contained a VCR (the most coveted electronic item *du jour*) and a note from "The Champ." During a lifetime in the sport, it was the only thank-you gift Gordon ever received from a grateful fighter, it remained a family keepsake for decades afterwards.

The portrait of the fighter at this point was of a diligent character shuttling between the gym and the chapel, while stopping occasionally to supplement his income.

"You know, I've never liked to fight. I still don't. I'm very religious, very Christian, don't like to hurt anybody. I am very skeptical about marriage. I don't believe in divorce. So I am still living alone. Sometimes I work out, usually I don't. Sometimes I work in the office of the salvage company, sometimes I don't."

In the ring, Berbick's first serious test came on April 3, 1979, against Bernardo Mercado, a Colombian with 21 wins and two defeats on his jotter. Ten thousand turned up to pack the Halifax Metro Center, a venue that had practically become his home stadium. Not that it proved advantageous for Berbick in any way that night.

He began the fight on the offensive, battering Mercado against the ropes early on. But he eased off to catch his breath and, with just seconds to go in the first round, Berbick dropped his left guard and Mercado connected with a right that knocked him out cold. Later, he would claim the loss was caused by emotional strain, a fight with an ex-girlfriend earlier that day leaving him in no state for combat.

"I still had it in my mind when I was fighting Mercado. I was thinking about it, but I still started the fight good and cut him up right after it started. I had him bleeding. Suddenly, I pull back and whack! It was the first time I was ever knocked out. I wasn't in bad shape, though. When I came to, all I wanted to do was fight."

That rather unique appraisal of what went wrong was corroborated by his camp, all of whom openly admitted he would have won except that he wasn't in the right mood. Most people who knew him understood and agreed with that rather prosaic assessment, and this became the knock on Berbick.

On the right day, he was capable of competing with anybody, or, depending on his mental state, liable to lose to anybody. Certainly, the reverse robbed his career of momentum. He fought four times over the next twelve months; his three wins included his annexing of the vacant Canadian heavyweight title and a lack-luster draw with journeyman Leroy Caldwell.

"This is a big country. I love Canada. I like being champion of Canada and I am proud to be a citizen of the Commonwealth. That is why I don't go to New York. Do you know the last time the Canadian heavyweight champion got a shot at the Commonwealth title? Nineteen thirty-five. I want to set the past straight for Canada. I'll stay as long as I can find sparring partners."

He had no choice but to stay because, as the summer of 1980 loomed, he was going nowhere. Slowly. In effect, he'd now become the type of fighter promoters covet when looking to place one of their recovering prospects on an undercard where he is almost guaranteed victory. Which explains why Don Kerr picked up the phone at his office in Halifax one day, and heard Bob Arum on the line, asking, "Do you still handle that bum Berbick?"

Opportunity was about to knock, in more ways than he could ever have imagined.

Sugar Ray Leonard and Roberto Duran were fighting for the WBC world welterweight title at the Olympic Stadium in Montreal on June 20, 1980. The Brawl in Montreal was supposed to be a co-promotion between Arum and Don King, but, attempting to put one over on his bitter rival, Arum had his own matchmaker pick the undercard fights without involving King in the process. He identified Berbick as a handy evening's work for John Tate, one of Arum's charges who was coming back from losing his WBA heavyweight title to Mike Weaver in Knoxville, Tennessee, three months earlier.

King's camp had been around the business long enough to see what was going down, and knew exactly how to retaliate. His matchmaker,

Bobby Goodman, recognized that this particular contest might be a chance to get revenge on Arum.

"We reached out to Berbick, set him up in camp, and got him some great sparring to get ready for an upset over Arum's contender [Tate]," said Goodman in Jack Newfield's *Only in America: The Life and Crimes of Don King*.

Their investment paid off handsomely.

Having had to face a lot more opposition than expected, an exhausted Tate lingered on his stool at the end of the eighth, as if contemplating staying there. When the bell finally tolled, he moved cautiously to the center of the ring. There, he met a newly-invigorated Berbick, who unfurled a thundering right to the head and followed that up with another strong left. Suddenly, bizarrely, his higher-ranked opponent turned around and tried to run for cover. As Tate shuffled away across the ring, Berbick chased him down, still throwing punches all the way. Finally, Tate came to rest, wrangled between the ropes within touching distance of a stunned Arum.

"Get up, sucka!" shouted Berbick. He didn't. He couldn't.

King was so taken with the theatrical way in which his plan to mess with Arum had come to fruition that he was cackling loudly, his arms raised in triumph just yards from where Tate remained entangled, his legs still twitching. Meanwhile, Berbick bounded dementedly around the ring with the delirium of a man who knew a single victory had changed forever the course of his career. Having plodded along with no great direction, now he would get a shot at dethroning Larry Holmes and, according to his own optimistic pre-fight calculations, earn his first million.

"I'm going to catch that world title," said Berbick in the ring. "Just give me a chance!"

King was in his ear a lot that night in Montreal, whispering that he represented his best chance of doing exactly that. The pair would have a tumultuous relationship for years after.

"I knew he wouldn't stay with us," said Tom McCluskey. "I'm not a genius but I knew it was time to get out. I know how King operates. That's too big-time for me."

McCluskey was speaking from bitter experience. Earlier in their relationship, Berbick briefly cast him aside when Archie Moore, former light-heavyweight champion and one-time trainer of George Foreman, had come calling. He knew King's brand of hyperbolic rhetoric could turn any fighter's head. So it proved. When Berbick signed on to face Holmes on April 11, 1981, it was a King production from top to bottom. And, with McCluskey gone, the new trainer was Lee Black, a veteran who'd started out as a cornerman in New York back in the mid-1950s, and who recognized Berbick's failings.

"With Trevor, somebody has to be in the corner making him fight," said Black. "You don't get the feeling he has the heart to destroy guys, to get rid of them. You really have to make him angry before he becomes vicious. If you didn't know Trevor and met him before a fight, you wouldn't bet twenty-five cents on that boy. I like a fighter with no doubts, full of confidence. But Berbick'd be saying, 'The other guy's a good fighter,' and you'd wonder. But that's just his way.

"Oh, Trevor has enough heart to fight. But a whole lot of fighters don't have the die-hard heart. There still are things we don't know about Trevor. He's never had a broken nose. Nobody's busted up his lip. If it does happen, how will he react? What path will he take? Trevor's not a seasoned fighter. He only had what, eleven fights as an amateur before he turned pro? He's still learning. He's a mix of a European and a North American fighter, and you can only take so much away from him, you can only remake him so much."

If his performance against the heavily favored Tate demonstrated he was an underdog capable of a bite more severe than his bark, his increased profile brought with it the money he craved. His purse for the Tate victory had been $30,000; the Holmes bout was worth $200,000, the sort of hike in income that prompted him to come up with a philosophy for his newfound wealth.

"Fighting is now my security," he said while being interviewed at his training camp in the Catskill Mountains. "I never want to work at those other jobs again. I try to be realistic in life. If you have a lot of money, you enjoy it and try to get more. But I invest it. I don't spend it foolishly. I've got five color TVs in my house, two with remote control. I get deals on them. I've got a three-bedroom house and I ordered a Mercedes Benz 450SL. I got good deals.

"I deal with a lot of rich people, and for some reason they don't want the label. They don't want to be called rich. I can't figure that out. But money isn't the only thing about this. I don't see Holmes as just a payday. This is a challenge to me, one of the things I set out to do. I want to impress myself. I respect Holmes. I say nice things about him now. That's part of my psychology. In the ring, Holmes will be saying, 'What happened to all that nigger's respect?'"

The more time the press spent with Berbick, the more they realized he was a complex character. It's not every fighter who, after sparring, would eschew the temptations of Vegas in favor of returning to his room to read the Bible.

"I like to keep in touch," he told reporters about a religious devotion he claimed started when he began having visions at the age of sixteen. What appeared to be almost a quirk at this point in his career, his faith would become more worrying later in life when accompanied by increasingly troubled behavior and diatribes. All that was a long way off, though, as he readied himself for his shot at glory.

"I have a chance to shake the world one more time," said Berbick. "I don't have a lot of people protecting me like Holmes and some fighters. I'm going in there on my own. I have to prove to myself I'm capable of boxing with Larry Holmes. People say I've got nothing to lose. They don't consider my pride. This is a personal thing. My dignity says to me, 'You are something.' I have got to win. If I don't, I haven't proved anything. Sure, the public might say that Berbick put up a good fight and blah blah blah. I've got to live with that. I've got to live with the fact that Larry Holmes beat me. I can't live with that."

Holmes went into the fight with a 36 and 0 record that included 27 knockouts. He was such a prohibitive favorite that he was already provisionally booked to take on Leon Spinks just five weeks later. Very few pundits expected Berbick to take him the distance; one newspaper even went deep into the book of boxing clichés and decried him as "a tomato can." Canadian television passed on the rights to the show, and it was almost impossible to find a Vegas bookie willing to accept a wager on it. Holmes was also peeved that so many "big-shot reporters" didn't bother even covering the fight, an insult to the esteemed office he held.

"Berbick's so different to most fighters," said Black, offering more insight into his charge. "He gets wound up, can't relax when he's training. Before the Tate fight, we had to get a woman to stay with him. Not for sex. Just to relax with her. All the trainers say to stay away from women but it was good for him. Nobody really knows about Berbick. He could be great. He needs a win here to prove that. It's very hard to measure his talent. He hasn't had the type of fight to bring it out. This is his shot."

He started the contest like a man determined to make the most of that shot.

"C'mon, try to hit me," shouted Berbick in the first round. "Come out here. I ain't no Ali."

He "wasn't no Ali"... in, oh, so many ways. But he was young, fit and game. He broke his thumb in the first round, which affected his left hook throughout. Yet, early in the second he continued his tactic of taunting Holmes, "Come on baby, come on and fight." The brazen attitude rattled the champion, and he appeared to lose his composure more than once. At a number of intervals, a large portion of the 4,500 at Caesars Palace Sports Pavilion were so taken with the underdog's pluck that they began to chant his name.

Eddie Futch was working Holmes's corner that night, a man experienced enough to witness a few rounds of this drama before offering some wise counsel to his fighter. "This kid's not going anywhere,"

Futch told Holmes. "Just settle down and box him, take the decision." Which is exactly what he did.

A couple of judges gave Berbick four rounds, and the consensus ringside was that he'd given Holmes a lot more than he or anyone else had bargained for. The champion admitted he hadn't expected to go the full fifteen, and described his opponent as "the strongest fighter I've ever met." In a very respectable defeat then, Berbick had established himself as a credible presence on the heavyweight scene.

"All week I said I was going to put up a good fight. I knew Larry wasn't going to stop me. There was no doubt about that. I goofed off a little too much," said Berbick. "I made a few mistakes. But I am young. I feel good. I think I belong as a legitimate contender. I'll be back. I want to show myself more in America."

Perhaps giddy with his newfound fame and increased earning potential, he told reporters he was considering purchasing property in Los Angeles.

"The money is popping up all over the place, and right now I am in a very contented position," said Berbick. "Nobody's going to move me and it's up, up from now on. By Christmas, I want to be a millionaire. It's there and I don't see why not."

The reality was a little different. His next time out, he fought Conroy Nelson at the Halifax Metro Center with both the Canadian and Commonwealth titles (that had been recently stripped from England's John L. Gardner) on the line. His purse was 27 percent of the gate, which turned out to be $25,000. If that was perhaps a little less than he expected—6,000 paid in—he dispatched Nelson inside two rounds with some style. This made him the first fighter representing Canada (Berbick was not a citizen, his official status was that of "landed immigrant") to be champion of the Commonwealth since Tommy Burns eight decades earlier.

"The title will never go back to England," said Berbick, obviously proud of his adopted country. "I am the greatest fighter in the Commonwealth. No one will take my crown from me as long as I am around. I will whip anyone around. I am an example for all the kids in Canada. I will fight anyone for the right type of money after this. Did you see that last punch? I knew there was no way he would get back up. I'm going to win the world's title and bring it to Canada and keep it here."

During the buildup to the victory over Nelson, rumors abounded that Berbick wasn't as diligent in his preparation as he might have been. Even his own camp was worried about his lackadaisical approach to sparring. He openly admitted there was some truth to that, but explained it was because his faith had distracted him. Having recently spoken before a gathering of 8,000 Christians at Prince Edward Island, his immediate concern after disposing of Nelson was getting himself ready to address a crowd three times that size at a forthcoming Billy Graham rally in Calgary.

"What is important is that I have re-consecrated my life to Christ. He told me, take up my cross and follow, and I did. And I found happiness and peace in my life. That is the most important thing in my life, not the fight and the money. I am more interested in those things… that Christ is using me. Everything is falling into place. Everything is coming naturally to me."

Within a few weeks, "everything" was about to include a rendezvous with Muhammad Ali.

CHAPTER FOUR
The Talk of Tinseltown

I've got just enough to carry me through the year and destroy Norton. Then I'm going to retire. Frankly, I'm nowhere near what I was a while ago.

Muhammad Ali, Munich, May 24, 1976

ON SEPTEMBER 16, 1981, THE eyes of the world were on Caesars Palace, Las Vegas. The long-awaited meeting of Sugar Ray Leonard and Thomas Hearns had been billed as "The Showdown," and everybody who purported to be anybody was in town for the occasion. Among the nearly 24,000 shoehorned into the temporary stadium constructed in the parking lot of the casino were a host of luminaries from showbiz and sports; Jack Nicholson was sitting with John Huston, John McEnroe in a suit and tie was next to Vitas Gerulaitis, Richard Pryor and Burt Reynolds, Larry Holmes and Gerry Cooney.

Even amid that galaxy of stars, one shone brightest. As Muhammad Ali walked through Caesars, heads turned and fingers pointed, just like they always did. When he strolled the temporary path through the tennis courts—with typical Vegas grandiloquence it had been named Appian Way—word started to filter through to the arena about his arrival. By the time he was taking his ringside seat, his presence was announced over the PA system and the crowd gave him a standing ovation. Others had been heralded in similar fashion that night, but his reception was the loudest and the longest.

A wonderful welcome, but it must also have been somewhat bittersweet. Here was Leonard, a twenty-five-year-old, facing down Hearns, twenty-two, for the undisputed welterweight championship of the world, and for guaranteed purses of $8 million and $5.1 million, respectively. There was no doubt now that Ali was no longer the biggest show in town. The circus had moved on to other acts. The heavyweight division had been eclipsed. A generation of lighter men who'd come to define an era in the sport had emerged. They earned huge purses, and their contests were appointment television across the globe. Just like Ali's used to be.

That the shameless old ham in him was hurt by this is obvious from some of the stuff he said about the younger, lighter fighters over the next few weeks. For all the adulation visited upon him by the fans in Vegas that night, there was a growing sense he resented the spotlight now being trained on other fighters rather than him, especially at a time when he had to struggle to find some place even willing to allow him box. He wouldn't be the first or last aging boxer to resent those who came after him, earning more and building on the foundations he'd laid.

It wasn't as though Ali had completely lost the ability to hog the limelight. Even after the date with Berbick had been confirmed for December 11, he had to interrupt the early stages of a badly-needed training camp to go to Asia. Long before James Cornelius pulled off his miracle, Ali had committed to an engagement in Hong Kong, a sapping trip for anybody, much less for a boxer working to get fighting fit. Everybody made the best of the arrangement by setting up some promotional events in Los Angeles upon his return.

These offered a glimpse of how much wattage Ali's star retained. A press conference was called for the Beverly Wilshire Hotel on October 30. Unfortunately, that turned out to be the day the recently-crowned Los Angeles Dodgers were having their World Series parade. Cornelius and others involved wondered if they could compete with that sort of rival attraction. How many of the local media would be otherwise engaged covering the baseball celebrations and festivities?

Their concerns were misplaced. Just about every sports hack in town turned up to hear Ali; the room at the Beverly Wilshire was full. In Tinseltown, it seemed, Ali's star had just enough of the old sparkle left. The name alone could still draw a crowd even if, it soon became apparent, many of the journalists present seemed to prefer that he wasn't there promoting a fight.

The emcee for the occasion was Shelly Saltman, a veteran sports promoter who had been brought in to help pull the fight together. With a lengthy and diverse resume that ran from the Ali-Frazier fights to Evel Knievel's failed attempt at jumping Snake River Canyon, Saltman's involvement denoted that more heavy hitters had now gotten on board the promotion. When Ali took his place on the dais alongside Trevor Berbick—and Thomas Hearns and Greg Page, who'd both signed on for the undercard—the prospect of a night of boxing in the Bahamas suddenly seemed a lot more plausible.

But before any of the fighters could speak, Saltman introduced the man who made it all possible.

"The promoter of the fight, the president of Sports Internationale Limited of the Bahamas, and that's with an e," said Saltman, "the gentleman who convinced Muhammad Ali that this must be the way to go and the place to do it is in the Bahamas, I'd like to introduce you to Mr. James Cornelius."

In a gray suit with a white shirt and a beaming smile, Cornelius rose diffidently from his seat next to Ali and, in his first exposure to the public, protested he wasn't expecting to say anything. Then he offered the following: "I'm very proud to be here on behalf of Sports Internationale Bahamas Limited, and very proud to be associated with Muhammad Ali. Thank you."

It was short and sweet, but it was obvious now that Cornelius was no longer lurking in the shadows, trying to orchestrate affairs from behind the scenes where, he hoped, the FBI and various other creditors couldn't track him down. No, he had, rather brazenly, become the front man for the whole operation and would, for better and for worse, retain that role until the end.

Next up was somebody else the journalists assembled had never heard of: Cyril Ijeoma, the Bahamian accountant who'd helped Cornelius float the idea of having a fight in Nassau. Now, he was being billed as a director of Sports Internationale.

"Ladies and gentlemen, it's a great pleasure for me to be here and to welcome you all to this momentous occasion. I would wish on behalf of Sports Internationale The Bahamas Limited to really thank the government and people of the Bahamas for having given us the opportunity to grant to Muhammad Ali his greatest desire, which is to win the championship of the world for the fourth time. It has been a very long road since the day James Cornelius came to see me in Nassau, and it's a great pleasure indeed to know that at long last we will have all of us there."

To further enhance the belief this was for real, Saltman gave the floor to Lionel Schaen of Select TV and John Ettlinger from Medallion Films, who were handling the domestic and worldwide distribution for the fight. Fresh off his involvement in the Hearns-Leonard fight, Schaen claimed that none of the promotional events ahead of that contest had drawn a press conference as well-populated as this one. Ettlinger sounded a more cautionary note, pointing out with a wry smile that it had taken a long while to put the negotiations to bed, and how tired everyone was from negotiating.

After cameos from Prentis Byrd (subbing for the unavailable Emanuel Steward), Thomas Hearns (answering questions about his decision to move up to middleweight for the first time on the undercard), and Greg Page (the up-and-comer from Louisville fighting on the same bill as the town's most famous fighter for the first time), Berbick was introduced as the Canadian heavyweight champion, ranked number seven in the world. He ambled to the microphone, wearing a cream suit, white shirt, and brown striped tie, handkerchief nestling in his top left pocket.

"Good morning ladies and gentlemen, it's a privilege to be here," he said, speaking more softly than you'd expect from such a big man.

"Lookin' forward to this extra special show that's gonna be in the Bahamas."

Then he beamed an awkward smile and gripped the lectern as his eyes scanned the room, like a man who'd never been in front of a microphone in front of an audience of this size before. Which, of course, he hadn't. Eventually, Shelly Saltman helped him out. "Any questions for Trevor?"

From the floor, he was asked if there was any chance he'd be overawed by getting in the ring with Ali?

"It's very hard to fight a man like Muhammad Ali, the fact he's a legend, a genius in the ring," said Berbick. "You say it, he's done it. I'm a young man who is out there to prove I have a chance. I'm gonna fight the greatest and I'm looking forward to a good show, it's going to be a good fight."

Would you be content with a close decision or you going for a knockout?

"I'm going to take whatever I can get. You go in there, you try and be happy with whatever I comes up with. Ali didn't train hard for the Holmes fight, but I know he's ready for this fight. If he defeats me, one of the world champions will have to fight him then, Weaver, Holmes or Cooney, whoever has it then will have to fight the man, there'll be a big showdown."

He delivered the last line with a flourish and the audience laughed. Even Ali's shoulders shook as he enjoyed the moment. That was the tone for the day. No faux snarling for the cameras. Not even the slightest hint of manufactured rancor. Ali beamed at him as Berbick left the dais, the gaze more that of a father looking upon his son, not a future opponent staring down his foe.

When it came to the main man, Saltman recited some of his own history with Ali, going back fifteen years and mentioning what a great champ he had been. Then, he referenced the elephant in the room, challenging any reporters who might have questions about Ali's fitness to fight to read the doctor's report that would be made available to them. That the promoters felt this was a necessary step perfectly captured how much opposition was growing to the prospect of Ali donning gloves again.

"But we don't need all that," said Saltman, the old pro slipping back into PR speak. "Because on December 11 you will see the man himself prove or try to prove that Muhammad Ali deserves the appellation given to him years ago—The Greatest! Ladies and Gentleman, Muhammad Ali!"

When he stood up, Ali looked good in a black suit, white shirt, and black tie. But when he started to speak, the delivery was slow, not drawn out like a vinyl record played at the wrong speed, yet definitely labored.

"Many people want to know why am I doing this? I say, why? Because it is there. Why did we go to the moon? Because it's there. We're not satisfied, now we're mapping out a plan to Mars. Why? Why Mars? Ain't the moon far enough? Mars because it's there and there's the possibility and chance of us reaching it. Why am I coming back? Because it's there, he's there and he can be got. And the four time championship can be got. But…we've defeated already so many critics, we've defeated so many promoters, so many governors, so many boxing commissioners. Already we see victory. When the power structure of this boxing country, when they say, 'No, we close the door and you finished,' they forgot that they said no to Muhammad Ali. They said no to [he pauses here for effect and goes down a couple of octaves before delivering an old classic] the greatest of all time."

The familiar line caused the room to erupt in a mixture of laughter and applause. Ali drank in the response then continued to call out the naysayers.

"They retired me. Now, after all I done for boxing, fighters can ask for $10 million. We want $12 million, we want $5 million. They couldn't even ask for $1 million until I started raising prices and making people come to boxing. All of a sudden, they going to retire me, the professor of boxing, the prophet of boxing, the resurrector of boxing! You gonna tell me I'm through, some flat-bootyed commissioner? Ain't no shape, or left jab going to tell me I'm through. They say I'm old. Do I look old to you?"

At which point he started preening himself, to the delight of the crowd. Smiling faux bashfully, he went on. "I know I'm pretty. But let me tell you something, I love controverse [sic]. Don't tell me no, You tell me no, I can't do it. I tell you you're a liar."

Like a great orator trying to persuade a skeptical audience, he dialed back the clock and took the room on a trip down memory lane. That everybody present knew the story and many of them had, indeed, accompanied him on the journey he had made didn't matter to Ali. He was on a roll.

"When I first came on the scene with Sonny Liston, my friend Greg [Page] was a little boy then, they said he can't do it, he'll kill the kid. Came in, stopped Liston, he stayed on his stool. The bell rung, his trainer said, 'Sonny the bell rung.' He said, 'My momma didn't raise no fool, I'm staying on this stool.' Then you know the rest, Vietnam fight, resist the draft. Said it was unjust war, it wasn't right, I was a bad nigger then but I turned out right because the war turned out wrong. Joe Frazier, I got knocked down, Norton, got my jaw broke. Came back, got Frazier two more times, got Norton two more times. Then came Leon Stinks, I mean Spinks, fight went fifteen rounds, did the rope a dope, thought he'd run out of gas, he's twenty-four years old, I'm thirty-seven, I'm gonna let him work himself out, thought he'd run out of gas but he didn't. So I lost the fight and told them I'm coming back. After all that happened, I went to my training camp, chopped trees and said, 'I'm coming back dancing, I'm not through.' Came back, danced fifteen rounds….

"Larry Holmes, I went 251 to 217 in eight weeks, lost the weight, quit eating sugar, quit eatin' salt, had no energy, lost the fight. Now they know I'm finished. Right? So here I stand today. They told me I couldn't get a license. We got a license, we got it first in Columbia, South Carolina, of all places. They told me I couldn't get an opponent, we got an opponent. Who you going to fight champ? My manager says, 'Going on forty, been off a year, take Franklin Thomas [he presumably meant Pinklon Thomas] or [Scott] LeDoux, or somebody to warm up on.' I'm too great to go out fighting bums."

Then he offered a deeper explanation for his choice of opponent, one that uncannily predicted exactly what would happen after the Berbick fight.

"Supposed I go fight a Joe Blow and he look good and I look bad. I can see him now [slips into note-perfect Howard Cosell impression]: 'It is a shame, Muhammad Ali was so great at one time, who would think he would stoop so low to fighting nobodies? Look at this great man now scuffling against the ropes.'

"I said, 'Find me the baddest man next to Holmes. Who's the baddest?' They said. 'Trevor Berbick.' I said, 'What, who's he?' I really didn't know him. 'From Canada? Canadian?' I said, 'I aint' fightin' no white fighters!' 'He's from Canada,' they said, 'and he 'ain't white, he is black, black, black!'"

The gags kept coming. The good-humored nature of the press conference was more suited to an exhibition bout than the prelude to a serious contest. Still, having lampooned Berbick, he then started to big him up for the audience.

"We saw film of him fightin' Holmes. He was on Holmes, he had Holmes shook up. He stopped Holmes's knockout record, boy. He put a whuppin' on, talking to him, saying, 'Come on Larry, come on Larry, come on Larry.'"

That Berbick had talked trash to Holmes was true. That he had put any kind of a whuppin' on him was not.

"Don't talk to me like that, please," said Ali, turning to Berbick, the pair of them grinning. "Don't have me in the ring laughing. Please be serious. Anyway, he gave Holmes all hell. I said, 'I want him, get him.' They said, 'You crazy, you don't have to prove nothing.' I said, 'I don't want to fight two or three people, training as hard as I am for this fight, get me the best fighter you can.' And here you are."

At which point he pivoted to pay respect to Berbick and to turn him into a comic foil.

"I want to thank you for fighting me under the pressure you've been under. I hope you've enjoyed your career."

The audience dissolved into laughter at the latest jibe, and Ali stopped to savor their response. Then he invited questions. The first concerned his willingness to fight Frazier if he managed to defeat Berbick.

"Frazier? Frazier's too old! [Cue more guffawing from the reporters and everyone else in the room.] He's four years younger than I am [sic]. No, not Frazier. My plans are to fight here, stay in condition, and I know people who have money and who can put their hands on seats. The reason I'm still so powerful, I still draw, and I deserve another chance. I can go to Russia, Indonesia, England. Wherever I go, I draw. I'm too powerful for them to stop me because they don't think I should fight. They can't stop me because I still draw too much money."

As the press conference wore on, the longer Ali spent on his feet it seemed that his speech deteriorated. Not in a way that made him difficult to understand, but just enough so that anybody who'd watched him over the years couldn't help noticing. That he was delivering stream of consciousness answers possibly didn't help combat that impression. Witness the choppy response to a question about his future plans:

"After this fight, I'll sit back and let the lawyers negotiate. They better get the biggest arena with the most seats, because there will be a terrible…. When I come back for the fourth time…. Boxing went 120 years before Floyd Patterson went twice. That was big news—two-time champion. After two-time champion looked so great, four-time champion is just impossible. See, when I was young, that wouldn't be so difficult, but now that I'm older the impossible is going to take a little while."

At this point, a journalist raised the issue of whether his motivation to keep going had less to do with fistic history and more to do with finances.

"You always need money. Rolls-Royce is trying to sell cars. Everybody trying to make a little money. Can't live without the money. But if I was just going for the money then I wouldn't have no faith in myself that I could actually do what I planned and not to get hurt. I'd go out looking bad for life, so the money can't pay for my pride, my name, my image in boxing, how people look at me. So I wouldn't do it just for the money."

He paused, as if unhappy with his own answer or trying to gather his thoughts. For a second he looked almost somber before taking his voice up a couple of octaves and regaining his flow.

"I'm going to be the first black image that nobody can top. See, you white people have a way of brainwashing the world. Jesus Christ, he's a white man, it's established. The world sees Jesus as a white man, blond hair, blue eyes."

To help the audience, he puts his arms out in a crucifix shape before continuing with a speech, variations of which he'd been giving for years. On this occasion, though, the delivery was a lot more staccato than the lyrical tirades about racial inequality he'd offered up in his pomp.

"The last supper, everybody's white, no black angels, no black people setting the table, no Chinese or Cubans either at dinner, all white folks, that's established, people believe that's the last supper, brainwashed the world. I didn't mean to get into this. Tarzan, he's the king of Africa, white man king of the jungle."

Again, he segued into a Tarzan impression. Miming the way he used to hold a rope over his head, he pretended to swing from tree to tree, and let out the famous Johnny Weissmuller call to the animals.

"You got the world believing Tarzan is the king of Africa. You telling us the white man is the king of the jungle. Wonder Woman is white. Superman white. Batman white."

He stopped, turned to Cornelius sitting next to the lectern.

"What color The Incredible Hulk?" he asked in a voice loud enough for everyone to hear.

"Green," said Cornelius.

"Oh," replied Ali, pausing for a laughter break, before restarting his rant. "Then you got the White Owl cigars? White Swan Soap, the White House. I'm dreamin' of a white Christmas. Angel food cake white, Devil food cake chocolate. Snow white."

The rant had the crowd rolling in the aisles.

"I'm serious, I'm tellin' you what's in my mind. That's why I'm here. Just the idea of coming up and doin' something all the white people say can't be done. And then to be bigger than Superman. To be bigger than Batman. To be bigger than Wonder Woman and all the white images. Then we'd have a black image more super than all of it—in real life! Your images are made up, fake images. This is a real image. Bigger than the World Series. I'll be bigger than everything you can make up. That's what I'm shooting for."

Riled up now, he wagged his finger at the audience and started to sound like a cross between a politician on the stump and a motivational speaker trying to change lives. Or at least a very choppy fusion of both.

"I got too many motivations. Too many black people, white too, give up too easy. People go, 'Crime is a big problem in the cities, black people got no jobs, can't persevere, can't wait for jobs, they give up too easy.' Somebody's wife or husband leave 'em, and they get sick, get ulcers, get cancer, kill themselves, instead of going out to find another one, they go crazy. See, people need motivation. You tell me I can't do it. You make me want to do it!"

The voice changed again, sounding almost child-like as he bounced on his two feet. "I got the whole world where I want 'em. I got all of you where I wantcha. I got the whole stage set. I love this. Don't tell me I can't do it, then I'll do it."

There followed a non sequitur, a very garbled revisiting of his earlier comments about Spinks, Norton, and Frazier before he regained his train of thought.

"Tell me I can't be a black Muslim and change my name in a white country, that made me do it. I love controversy. I love drama. This is a perfect set… I got all the suckers set up."

In a voice shrill with excitement, he waved his right hand back and forth to emphasize the point he was trying to make. "All the suckers are set up."

For a moment, the journalists were in the palm of his hand and he knew it. Pausing for dramatic effect, he lowered his voice, buttoned his jacket and said, "That's all I'm saying for now. Bye…" And then he made to walk off the stage. After such a mixed performance in front of the microphone, here was the Ali of old, the actor possessed of the kind of comic timing that cannot be taught.

The assembled fighters posed for the photographers then. As Ali stood alongside Hearns, Page, and Berbick, he was talking continuously. Hearns pretended to be trying to separate the headliners and Ali, the most experienced model, took Berbick's right hand, placed it on his own chin, and asked, "Did you call me a nigger?"

Berbick laughed uproariously, Page pretended to hold Ali's right fist back, and the three-time champion continued to ham it up. "Nigger, did you call me a nigger?" The crowd was enjoying it, and Ali, relishing the spotlight and the cameras flashing in his face, kept up the shtick. "He called me black! Who you callin' black?"

There were more photographs with well-wishers who swarmed him, and another round of publicity shots. The usual follies. Eyeballing Thomas Hearns, joshing with Berbick, one moment pretending to punch him, the next shaking his hands. When the media obligations were fulfilled, Ali then sat on a rather bizarre throne to record a promotional video in which he was asked many of the same questions as earlier in the day. However, some of the inquiries and his responses offered an insight into how different this entire production was.

For instance, he offered up a bizarre theory about his best fighting weight.

"Fighting, I hope to weigh about 233. I gotta be heavy, I have to face it, the teens is too light. That was for when I was a kid, a teenager myself. My bones are heavy. I was too light when I fought Holmes, I had no energy. I couldn't win one round. I gotta get myself sharp and strong and, with weight, about 233 or 235. But I gotta get myself in shape. If Holmes was the best I can do I should retire. In a fifteen-round fight we can lose eight to ten pounds that night, and if I'm 217 I have no energy to burn."

And then this about his medical condition, during which he mixed up the different clinics he'd visited.

"I went to UCLA medical center and got on all the machines, kidney, brain, thyroid, urine, blood, all kinds, for three days. And they says, Doctor Demopoulos, he says, 'A-1.'"

Demopoulos was actually a pathologist at New York University Medical Center, which is obviously what Ali meant to say.

"That wasn't enough. I went to UCLA medical center, Dr. Cope, check it out, Dr. Cope, laid on all kinds of machines, checked everything again. That wasn't enough. Then I went to Mayo Clinic. The boss of all clinics, the Mayo Clinic, stayed two days, A-1. They got all kinds of rumors that I'm not in shape. I got brain damage. Do I sound like I have brain damage?

"You've been talking to me. I'm handling your questions. Didn't I tell you before this interview, 'Don't show me no questions?' The man brought the questions over to me. And says, 'Prepare yourself.' I said, 'No, catch me off guard!' Ain't that true? That show what kind of brain damage I got. I got more sense than anybody. Who can handle you like I'm handling you now? Brain damage! What's your question?"

And how did he intend to approach the fight?

"My plan is to dance, to dance in and out. It's only but ten rounds. If I win seven, even six of the rounds on all judges' cards, it's my fight. Dancin' all night, stickin' and movin' and dancin'…[as he spoke he issued flurries of punches replete with sound effects] All night! On my toes! All of you forty-year-old men are gonna be proud after this fight. All of you old men, they tell you you're forty and you think you're finished, and you're washed up. As they say, life begins at forty if you live right. And my fans, man, before I left the Bahamas last week, to test my speed, I cut the light off in my bedroom, I hit the switch, I was in bed before the room was dark."

After the flourish of that old line often attributed to Satchel Paige, the legend of Negro League baseball, he was brought down to earth with a question about his third wife Veronica's view of the fight.

"How do my wife feel? She wish I don't. But she's with me if I'm gonna do it. She wish I don't. She tried to talk me out of it, but it's impossible."

And what if you lose?

"If is a helluva word. If I had a billion dollars I'd be a billionaire. If! If you was handsome, you wouldn't be ugly. If! So I don't think like that. That would be a disaster to lose. It never really comes across my mind. I just can't imagine me losing. No, man, I ran six miles this morning. I'm getting trim, I'm in shape. I'm the same Ali [throwing punches again, more percussive sound effects]. Fast as I ever was. I had a bad night with Holmes. I was just sick that night.

"I know I can still go. I wouldn't embarrass myself and my family and my whole image and my religion by goin' out getting hurt. I love myself more than you do. What people care about me more than me? I analyze this whole thing and I'm gonna win. I'm still ready. I'm ready! Whose idea was it that I'm dumb and somebody talked me into it? And they pushed me into the gym every day, push me to run every day. Man, this is my idea!"

For all the tough talk and the reworking of some of his greatest verbal hits, one or two journalists were starting to get a whiff that all was not as it seemed to be. Eschewing the party line as per the press conference that everything was good to go, Allen Abel of the *Toronto Globe and Mail* made some exploratory phone calls to the Bahamas. He spoke to a reporter on the ground in Nassau who'd witnessed some of Ali's early workouts. The bulletin was not inspiring.

"It's just going to be a big show, a put-on fight." said Steve McKinney. "He says he wants to weigh 225 pounds for the fight, but he's still at 242, so he'll probably start taking that medicine again that made him sick in Las Vegas. We don't know how many tickets have been sold. How many people here have a thousand dollars?"

Abel also worked his contacts in Canadian boxing, and Don Kerr, former manager of Berbick, told him that the people involved in the promotion would never be able to underwrite the purses being mentioned. That sounded like sour grapes from somebody who'd lost his biggest fighter and largest cash cow. But Kerr's comments would sound very prescient very soon.

CHAPTER FIVE

Searching for the Fountain of Youth

As of now, I am quitting boxing. And will devote all my energy to the propagation of the Muslim faith. Mark my words and play what I say right now fully. At the urging of my leader Wallace, I declare that I am quitting fighting as of now and from now on I will join in the struggle of the Muslim cause. I have defeated everyone in the world in my time. I have a record I challenge any boxer after myself to match. And I have decided I should retire.

Muhammad Ali, Governor's office, Istanbul, October 1976

SHORTLY AFTER THE BOUT WITH Trevor Berbick had been arranged, Muhammad Ali phoned the home of José Torres. The former light-heavyweight champion-turned-author was scheduled to interview him for a feature in the December issue of *Sport* magazine.

"Who is calling?" asked Torres's wife, Ramonita.

"The greatest fighter in the history of the world," said Ali.

The Puerto Rican native had a unique history with Ali. He was a boxing contemporary of his in the 1960s and, indeed, at a luncheon had once famously challenged Ali to take him on.

"C'mon man, you and me," taunted Torres. "I need a good payday. We'll pack them in."

Rather than respond directly, Ali looked at Ramonita and said wryly, "You have to feed him a lot of rice and beans. Only then can I make money for your man."

In 1972, Torres published *Sting Like a Bee*, a well-received biography of Ali, written from his own distinctive perspective as peer, friend, and, later, objective journalistic observer. During their lengthy sit-down ahead of the Berbick fight, Torres, who fought for the last time at the age of thirty-three, didn't hold back. He asked pertinent questions that prompted some honest answers.

Ali reiterated again that Veronica didn't want him to fight, confessed that he didn't have the same coordination as before, and, perhaps most tellingly, admitted he wouldn't want his son, Muhammad Jr., to ever get in the ring.

"Too dangerous. Too savage. Too risky. I want him to be educated and be a doctor or a lawyer. Or an interpreter to speak the truth and learn many languages. Or a government official or a politician. Anything but sports, because that's my life's history."

Torres raised the constant rumors Ali was now regularly slurring his speech. Once more, he denied this.

"Only when I'm tired. When I got tired they caught me in a couple of instances where I was slurring my speech. I was lazy. I didn't feel like talking. But right now, as I'm talking to you this moment, I'm sure you can tell that I'm talking as good and as proper as anybody that's ever been hit on the head."

Torres also repeatedly asked Ali about the wisdom of going to the well one more time.

"I can still do the same things I used to do, but I have to plan better," said Ali. "I just can't do things on the spur of the moment. We have to work longer, not harder. Where it used to take four weeks to get into shape, now it takes twelve. Instead of running three miles a day I might just run two miles, but for a longer time. Instead of boxing twelve rounds a day in a gym with the speed bag, heavy bag, ropes and shadowboxing, now I might cut to eight rounds. And instead of working one month straight in the gym, going twelve rounds, I might work six weeks doing eight rounds. You have to take a little out, put a little in, change this, change that."

If there at least seemed a weird sort of logic and some kind of mathematical equation to Ali's new philosophy of training, the reality of his preparation was proving to be somewhat different.

* * *

The clock had not yet ticked past five when Muhammad Ali rose from his bed in Suite 642 at the Britannia Beach Hotel and dressed for his morning run, his outfit including a rubber corset designed to encourage a thirty-nine-year-old body to shed excess sweat. In the foyer downstairs, he strolled past a gleaming white statue of himself under which was a notice bearing the message: "Britannia Beach Greets the Champion: This statue is comprised of 80 lbs of lard. Compliments of Chef Rolf Epprecht."

Nobody in management seemed to get the irony of this creation.

Outside, the temperature was already nudging its way into the low 50s, chilly for the Bahamas in November, but perfect conditions for an overweight boxer badly needing to pound the pavement ahead of an upcoming bout. Boxing journalists, newly arrived in Nassau, were concerned about his physical condition after more than a year out of the ring, but he assured them he'd been putting in three miles a day at a good clip for nearly two months. On this particular morning, three of the more intrepid reporters, including Hugh McIlvanney, then of London's *Observer* newspaper, had set their alarms to come see for themselves.

These men knew Ali in his prime. They knew him as the man who once famously declared, "The fight is won or lost far away from the witnesses, behind the lines, in the gym, and out there on the road; long before I dance under those lights." It was a quote so perfect and telling it was destined to hang forever on the walls of locker-rooms and gyms and wherever athletes needed reminding of the necessity of hard work and diligent preparation.

On this day, however, their reward for rising early was to witness an Ali more jiggly than rippling, struggling like a man approaching middle age (which is, of course, what he was), his heavy footfalls soundtracked by the crowing of roosters in the agricultural darkness beyond the main roads.

Almost as soon as his course took him up the incline of the Paradise Island Bridge, his breathing started to sound labored. After barely a mile the slow-motion jog eventually segued into a walk, and that was punctuated now and again by him stopping altogether to shadow-box, brandishing a weight in each of his hands. The punches thrown were, like the jogging that preceded them, being unfurled almost as if in slow motion.

On the streets of Nassau's shopping quarter, a young man came running towards the entourage and did a double-take at the sight of the most famous fighter in the world in his midst. He stopped and Ali began to playfully spar with him.

"What you doing here?" asked the delighted local. "You fighting again?"

Minutes later, with a lot less than two miles done and the sun now starting its ascent into the sky over the Caribbean, Ali climbed into a waiting limousine and headed back to his hotel, back to his bed.

"A man who has missed the last bus after the bars close takes more out of himself on the walk home than Ali had done with what we were supposed to regard as roadwork," wrote McIlvanney. The legendary Scottish scribe had witnessed Ali training in his prime, and he knew this was about as far removed from that warrior as it was possible to be.

"He not only loved doing his roadwork," said Angelo Dundee of his charge one time, "he knew it was the source of his stamina. So he would run until he was tired, sometimes running backward, and then he'd run some more—across causeways, up and down streets, and even over golf courses, cutting his legs on unseen sprinkler heads dotting the fairways; I'd have to treat his bloodied legs all the time. He used to worry the heck out of me. But bloody legs or not, he would run…"

That was then. Now, he was cheating on his mileage each morning and many of his training sessions in the afternoon lasted barely twenty minutes. The bizarre location for these workouts was Le Cabaret, the hotel dining room that each evening hosted a Las Vegas-style revue. The stage had to be cleared of the props, the backdrops lifted to the gods before curious locals could be charged $3 to come in to watch Ali work up a sweat in an improvised ring. Or, at least, go through the motions of doing so.

To witness Ali shadowboxing used to be one of the great privileges in sport. An up-close glimpse of an athletic marvel, a body perfectly tuned, a coil ready to spring. All that footwork. All that rhythm. Hands moving at the speed of blur. Head bobbing to avoid imaginary punches. If that was a wondrous sight worth any admission fee, this was something completely different.

The Bahamians who filed in each day deposited their cash in a shoe box on a card table. Most eschewed the chance to purchase "The Drama in the Bahamas" T-shirts being flogged near the door. Small yet significant details that reminded everybody the show wasn't playing the Vegas Strip anymore.

"Ladies and gentlemen, as you know, Muhammad Ali is in serious training for his upcoming fight with Trevor Berbick," said the hotel employee who would call the crowd to order. "It would be appreciated if you did not call out or do anything to break his concentration."

The grandiloquence did not become the occasion.

"He wears the look of a man in mindless ritual—jab, hook, dance, move—backward, always backward, bobbing and weaving against an opponent only he can see," wrote Canadian journalist Jim Taylor of what he saw at Le Cabaret. "The feet shuffle and slide, the breath snorts through the nose. There is no other sound. After the third round, he leans against the ropes in his corner, his back to the crowd, waiting while they hook up the heavy bag. 'I have returned, I have returned. I have returned!' He hasn't turned his head or moved anything but his lips. It's as though he's reading cue cards on the canvas at his feet. 'There's gonna be a miracle! Be among those who dare to dare!'…The lines are still there but the magic is missing."

Once Ali had satisfied the minimum requirements every afternoon, he'd don a robe, pull up a chair and really give the customers their money's worth with a question and answer session. They'd pepper him with queries about opponents, past rather than present, and he'd turn every one into a chance to talk up his future prospects. Witness the following exchange.

"What are you going to do after you regain the title?"

"Hold it for about five years!"

He often used that stage to mock those who derided his efforts, hammering, especially, unnamed people who spread rumors his brain and liver were severely damaged. Even if the back and forth often lasted longer than the training itself, and was far more entertaining.

"You are all my people!" Ali told the crowd. "Black, white, Chinese! They are all my people."

His daily routine culminated in a return to an empty dressing room behind the stage. There, he'd eat grapes and lie on a cot, surrounded by sequined dresses, pirate costumes, wigs, swords, and jars and all the other paraphernalia worn by those who performed at Le Cabaret's dinner show. The bizarre and diminished circumstances didn't lessen his braggadocio any.

"They say I'm old, I got bad kidneys. I can't get on TV," said Ali when a group of reporters sat with him after training one day. "They say I couldn't get the license. Why is everyone worried that a black man is going to get hurt? White people take risks all the time. Climb them mountains with those little picks. All I did for American boxing and they wouldn't give me a license. Fighters making $200 million now. I started that. I changed the whole picture and they ran me out. But I forgive them. They know not what they do."

His attempt at biblical magnanimity towards those who'd hindered his attempt to fight again was matched only by the quality of his name-dropping, which also served to remind everybody he was so much bigger than this sport and this off-Broadway locale.

"Three weeks after this fight, I've got to go to Peking. Deng Xiaoping wants me to introduce boxing to the Chinese people. Then I've got to go to Russia. (Leonid) Brezhnev's having something at Red Square. I've got to stand alongside him. If a journalist followed me, it would be incredible. Can you imagine me and Brezhnev having dinner, watching the tanks in Red Square?"

At a certain point in mid-November, it became a lot easier to picture Ali yukking it up with the General-Secretary of the Communist Party than to believe he'd ever make it into the ring with Berbick. Not through any particular fault of his own. He'd kept up his part of the bargain, decamping to the Bahamas and entering perhaps the most subdued and relaxed training camp of his career. The problem was that $100,000 due from James Cornelius and the promoters had not reached Ali's bank account, and this was enough to cause him to down tools and stop training altogether.

Cornelius was starting to feel the pressure on a number of fronts. The management of the Britannia Hotel also wanted some of the enormous bill being run up to be paid down sooner rather than later. A pressing concern but, obviously, nothing compared to the possibility of the star turn deciding this was no longer worth his trouble. In a private meeting, Cornelius tried to assuage Ali's worries and promised the money would materialize. After two decades around pro boxing, Ali didn't seem to share the neophyte promoter's confidence that he had the wherewithal to still pull this one off.

"While barely rearing his head," wrote Cornelius. "Ali told me, 'Ya know, promoting is hard stuff. Suppose someone put $200,000 in a briefcase for you and you forgot about this fight.'"

The increasingly paranoid Cornelius saw the hand of Don King in that cash offer, believing that the more experienced promoter was now waiting in the wings to capitalize on his misfortune and take over the whole event. Having asked his contacts in Ali's entourage to convince him to stay in Nassau, Cornelius went about trying to raise the missing money. By his own account, he solved the problem by selling a large chunk of Sports Internationale Bahamas Ltd to Tee Kay Shipping, a Nassau-based corporation involved in the transportation of oil around the globe, for $300,000. His dream was still alive, even it remained very much on life support.

In the meantime, word had percolated through American boxing circles that all was not well in the Bahamas, and doubts began to grow that the fight would ever happen. Bert Sugar, then editor of *The Ring* magazine, articulated this view in the media, and dubbed the bout "The Trauma in the Bahamas," a title that would stick. A New York travel agent, who'd put together a package called "The Nassau Knockout," offering return flight, four nights in a hotel and $5 in casino chips, admitted to a reporter that the sales were only moderate.

Reached at his training camp in the Catskill Mountains, where by all accounts he was a lot more committed to his preparations than his putative opponent, Trevor Berbick tried to rise above all the negativity.

"I'm sure it'll come off. I've got some money for it already. Ali got some, too. I don't believe he'd take the money and not fight. He wants to fight."

Berbick's sanguinity may have had its roots in his theory, also held by many others, as to what exactly was motivating Ali to fight again.

"It's only my opinion and it's based on hearsay, but I think all that money Sugar Ray and Hearns got for their fight began making Ali jealous."

The naysaying was brought to a temporary halt when Cornelius transferred $100,000 to Ali's account on November 23. Conscious of the need for damage limitation, the increasingly beleaguered promoter then asked him to hold an outdoor event at Rawson Square in downtown Nassau. In a plaza named for the Englishman who governed the Bahamas back in the 1860s, Ali gave an impromptu press conference at which he tried to assuage fears that the bout was going to be canceled.

"Did you get all the money?" asked one reporter.

"The money's up," said Ali. "But the principle of the thing is more important. I have to show up the experts who say I can't do it. For years, people have been telling me what I can't do and what I can do. And I always made them wrong. And I tell you now that anybody who says that I ain't going to be here December 11th in that ring with Berbick is lying."

The presence of Ali in the heart of the tourist area wowed onlookers, garnered some headlines, and definitely represented a public relations coup for Cornelius. But much more work needed to be done to generate interest in the fight back in America. To this end, Ali did a telephone interview with Red Smith, which was featured in the *New York Times* on the day after Thanksgiving.

"You can put in your article," said Ali, giving it the very hard sell, "I ain't had nothin' but victories, and we've overcome a lot of obstacles and the fight will come off, drawing thousands from all over the world. I finally got a license, and that's a victory. I got the best opponent against Holmes—Larry couldn't take him out—a victory. We got a select network. All the money is up, another victory. All the doctors at UCLA and Mayo' make me 100 percent healthy. I'm training great. I started at 249 pounds and I'm down to 230 1/2. I'm going up a little, to about 232. I was too light at 217 for Holmes. I was better at 230 for [Joe] Bugner."

Smith had once been one of Ali's fiercest critics, denouncing him as a "draft dodger" for his refusal to be inducted into the United States Army during the Vietnam War. By this point in his career, though, Smith sounded sympathetic to the way his former nemesis was raging stubbornly against the dying of the light. His attitude seemed to be that Ali was free to do as he wanted, and anybody who objected didn't have to watch. He certainly afforded him plenty of space to vent.

"The biggest thing is to show them I can still come out on top. I got to prove the experts wrong. I have to show I'm still the greatest of all time. I got four good sparring partners, two good cooks, a good massage man. Now all I need is to knock off Berbick to show the public I was sick against Holmes. They left me for dead. They said I couldn't fight anymore. They say I'm too old. Ain't no fighter in the world would have the power to do what I've done, what I'm about to do."

Some of that was true, but definitely not all of it. Witness the view of Jeff Stoudemire, one of those aforementioned sparring partners.

"I can't stop him," said Stoudemire, a light-middleweight journey-man with a 5 and 1 pro record. "He has his own mind, he's self-motivated somehow, but I feel that after this one he should call it quits."

Given that he'd worked in Ali's camp before the Holmes fight, Stoudemire didn't sound especially thrilled about his employer continuing to box. He and other lighter fighters were brought in, ostensibly to help Ali work on his speed. Although he also worked with an amateur heavy-weight named Tony Coster, who gave him all he could handle during one particular four-round session that dismayed watching reporters, those questioning the validity of the whole bout argued that Ali preferred the smaller opponents simply because they didn't hit him as hard.

Robert Folley's presence on the roster of sparring partners offered some historical perspective on the challenge facing Ali. A twenty-two-year-old welterweight out of Chandler, Arizona, his father Zora had fought Ali for the world heavyweight title at Madison Square Garden in 1967, gaining kudos for his bravery on the way to being knocked out in the seventh. Fourteen years on, here was one of Folley's sons helping his conqueror round into shape for one more tilt at the windmill.

If that type of footnote underlined just how long Ali had been on the go, there were other reminders, too. Lana Shabazz first met Cassius Clay when she worked at a Muslim restaurant in Manhattan in 1962, and had been cooking for him since after the Sonny Liston fight two years later. When the reporters came calling on her in Nassau, she toed the party line and talked up how great it was to see him back at work.

"It's fabulous that Ali is fighting again. With the whole gang together again, it's just like old times."

Asked what was different from previous adventures around the globe, Shabazz blurted out, "Well, one thing has changed, you know, Ali's hair is turning gray." Quickly realizing this was perhaps not something that her employer wanted to share with the world, she tried to correct herself, only to dig a deeper hole by implying his hair was being dyed to stave off one of the more tell-tale signs of aging. "The gray hair?" she said. "Don't worry about that kid. We're taking care of his gray hair, too."

There were plenty of other ways to gauge the passing of years. Thanksgiving week, he'd phoned the Dundee house in Miami and ended up talking to Angelo's daughter, Terri. She was twenty-four, and Ali asked her when she was getting married. As Angelo then pointed out, he first started calling their house when Terri was a little baby whose cries and wails interrupted their conversations. The bright, young Ali from those days was now weeks away from from turning forty and so obsessed with regaining his title that he peppered his trainer with questions about elderly champions like Archie Moore, Sugar Ray Robinson, and Jersey Joe Walcott.

Whether by accident or design, Dundee was also in the papers the day after Thanksgiving talking up his man's prospects, telling Bob Verdi in the *Chicago Tribune* that he "liked what I saw" during a brief trip to Nassau.

"Now people think I should force Ali not to fight. I would never do that. First of all, he's fighting this fight for himself. He beats Berbick, he doesn't win the championship. He just wins the Muhammad Ali Fountain of Youth Crown. He wants to fight this one just so he can prove to everyone that he's still got it. He's living for the moment when he can get up in that ring and point fingers at all the writers who buried him.

"I think it's gonna happen, too, and that's the other reason I would never tell him to quit. I watched him for a couple of days in Nassau, and he's working real good. His spirits are good, he's really motivated, but the key to this training is that he's put the scale away. That killed him the last time. There was no coal in his furnace. He spent so much time in front of the mirror he forgot about his energy. He thought light made right, so he went all the way down to 217 pounds. He had no strength, no stamina, no nothing."

After so long together, Dundee was being loyal to the extreme. What else could he say when he knew, regardless of his wishes, that Ali was determined to fight? Although Verdi correctly pointed out in his piece that Dundee was viewing the entire farrago through "rose-colored glasses," he gave him free rein to try to justify what was going down.

"When I saw him Wednesday he was about 230, which is where he'll stay. He's training against good quick sparring partners, and he's not worried about how pretty he is. Don't get me wrong. Ali is only half of what he used to be in his prime, but half is good enough to beat Berbick. Ali's still got the quickness in his hands, but not in the legs.

"He doesn't have the bounce and rhythm of ten years ago, but he can still walk at you and hurt you with combinations. I thought he'd win the Holmes fight and I think he'll win this one. I realize that a lot of people might think Muhammad is pathetic, and that he might drop dead right there in the ring, but if you don't believe me believe the doctors. He passed all his physicals."

And what of the increasing body of evidence that his speech was often slurred?

"He goes so many places and is always on stage," said Dundee. "That'll wear anybody out. The Ali I saw last week was sharp and alert. No slurs. When I go back there about December 6th, it'll be the same. He's ready. I've had nine champions, I know what I'm talking about. If he loses this fight and lays another egg, it'll be his last egg. But I want to be at the last hurrah if that's what it is. I'm not worried about Berbick or his health though. And don't tell me about the slurs. Don't you mumble when you're ready to go to sleep?"

Dundee's appraisal of where his man stood stands in marked contrast to the more objective opinion of his great contemporary Eddie Futch. When he arrived in the Bahamas to prepare Ernie Singletary for his fight with Hearns, Futch took in one of Ali's training sessions, and he didn't sugarcoat what he saw.

"It was slow motion," said Futch. "The jab had no snap. He didn't move. Four rounds of nothing and he was wore out. Ali is fighting. Joe [Frazier] is making that comeback because they see these young fighters and they see their deficiencies and they think they can whip them. But what they don't see is that their own reflexes ain't what they used to be. They see an opening but they can't deliver the punch. Or they can see a punch coming and they get hit with it when they wouldn't have before. They tell themselves, 'I'll be quicker next time,' or 'I'll be in better shape next time.' They're just refusing to believe what their body is telling them. It's like a pair of socks. When the elastic goes, it's gone. Throw the socks away. You can't fix the elastic. The reflexes are the elastic in your body. If it's gone, it's gone."

Futch knew Ali better than any trainer not named Dundee. He'd masterminded Joe Frazier's victory over him in 1971. Two years later, he was in the corner guiding Ken Norton when he got the better of Ali in San Diego. As a student and historian of the fight game, he was as shrewd a judge as was out there, and he reckoned Ali to be the best athlete of any fighter he'd ever seen. And now, he saw that athlete was in a state of disrepair.

"Of the great athlete, there's only one thing left. He can't circle anymore. He can't hurt you with any punch. He can't evade any punch by leaning away from it anymore. He can't take the body shots, but he still has the last good thing a fighter loses—the jab. The jab was the last thing Joe Louis lost. He kept Rocky Marciano off him for seven rounds with the jab [in a 1951 comeback at age thirty-seven]. But in the eighth, he got old in a hurry and Rocky got him good."

And what of Ali's chances?

"No way Ali can win this one unless Berbick fights a strange fight. Ali can't hurt him, and Berbick will tear him in two if he gets him on the ropes. Berbick is too strong for Ali now."

CHAPTER SIX

Doctors Differ, Patient Continutes to Fight

I'm using boxing for one more year. My fights are being carefully planned. I'm looking to take no more risks unless they pay me.
Muhammad Ali, Deer Lake, PA, August 20, 1977

DR. FERDIE PACHECO USED TO tell a story about the first time nineteen-year-old Cassius Clay visited his clinic at North West Second Avenue and 10th Street in the Miami ghetto of Overtown. It involved his long-serving nurse Mable Norwood chasing the elusive teenager around the treatment room, his pants around his ankles, as she tried to administer a shot. His fear of needles was such that he kept scampering just out of reach, trying to stay one step ahead of the dreaded jab.

"That child is either gonna end up in the crazy house or be champion of the world," said Norwood when the wayward patient had finally been pinned down.

In Overtown, Pacheco operated his clinic for medical more than financial reasons. Mendicant patients paid what they could afford, and if they couldn't afford anything at all, well, true to his oath, nobody was ever turned away. Over time, he also entered into an arrangement with Chris and Angelo Dundee at the 5th Street Gym who, in those days, often struggled to find quality and convenient health care for the black boxers on their books.

Pacheco treated all their fighters for free at his surgery, and his reward was a complimentary ticket to every bout in which the Dundees were involved. From there, it was a small step to becoming Ali's physician and having the media around the world christen him "The Fight Doctor." It was an impressive sobriquet, but one which doesn't quite do justice to a true Renaissance man, somebody who wrote novels and screenplays and later gave up medicine to become a full-time and highly-rated painter.

"What was it like to be Ali's fight doctor?" offered Pacheco of his role. "It was like being Queen Victoria's gynecologist. The title didn't mean much, but the view was spectacular."

In the early years of the relationship, the doctor didn't have much heavy lifting to do with this particular patient, a young man in the prime of his life. Truly, a sight to behold.

"When Ali was young, he was the best physical specimen I've ever seen," recalled Pacheco. "If God sat down to create the perfect body for a fighter, anatomically and physiologically, he'd have created Ali. Every test on him was a fine line of perfect. His blood pressure and pulse were like a snake. His speed and reflexes were unbelievable. His face was rounded, with no sharp edges to cut, and, on top of that, his skin was tough."

The physical toll his career began to take on him first manifested itself in Ali's hands. From 1970 onwards, Pacheco injected a combination of cortisone and Xylacene between his fingers before fights. Two shots per hand were designed to dull the pain he felt when punching. It was September 29, 1977, however, when the doctor realized Ali was taking too much punishment in bouts, and his difficulties were extending to other parts of his body. The epiphany came during Ali's sapping contest with Earnie Shavers at Madison Square Garden. He eked out a victory but absorbed far too many percussive blows while doing so.

"He won the fight," said Pacheco, "but his kidneys lost the decision."

Pacheco's suspicion that the time had come for Ali to stop was confirmed by a subsequent conversation with Dr. Frank Guardino of the New York State Athletic Commission. Guardino told him that Ali's lab work had come back showing blood in his urine (which had been a problem for quite some time), and other troubling signs of kidney damage. More than a decade after he first examined Ali, the medical evidence was enough for Guardino to declare he would never allow him another license to compete on his watch.

True to his word, the Shavers victory would be Ali's last appearance in a New York ring. And Pacheco? Well, he then faced a crisis of conscience that altered the course of his own life.

"I decided to write a letter explaining all our findings, the lab report and opinion of Dr. Guardino, and my strong recommendation that Ali not fight again," wrote Pacheco. "I added one thought. If he ever fought again, I would not be with him. I sent out five separate letters, certified mail, return receipt requested. They went out to Ali, Herbert [Muhammad], Angelo [Dundee], Veronica [Ali's wife], and Herbert's brother Wallace Muhammad, who was now head of the Muslims. It was no surprise that I did not receive one call or letter from anyone."

Pacheco walked away from Ali. He had nothing to gain from doing so. In fact, he gave up one of the best seats in sport, rather than be party to something he felt was no longer in the fighter's best interests.

"Hey doc, why you keep saying I'm all washed up?" asked Ali when their paths crossed in New Orleans before the second fight with Spinks a year later.

"I don't," replied Pacheco. "What I do say is you should not be fighting."

He left and he stayed away from the camp, if not the sport. But he didn't stop speaking out, telling anybody who'd listen that Ali's worst enemy was himself, and that nobody in his entourage had the power to get him to stop. Some, like promoter Bob Arum, accused Pacheco of being excessively dramatic with his pronouncements. In the aftermath of the Holmes debacle, by which time more and more people had gravitated towards Pacheco's side of the argument, he went into great detail about why Ali needed to hang them up.

"I just don't want him to fight anymore," said Pacheco. "In two or three years, we'll see what the Holmes fight did to his brain and kidneys. That's when all the scar tissue in the brain will further erode his speech and balance. That's when the thirty to forty bruising body shots will take the toll on his kidneys. He was a damaged fighter before the fight, and now he's going to be damaged even more....The people around him need to make him think straight. That's where the responsibility lies....The Ali we saw Thursday night wasn't the Ali who had a heart the size of the Empire State Building. He didn't fight at all. He just took his $8 million and got out."

Fittingly then, as the Berbick contest loomed into view, Pacheco wasn't holding back.

"Ali looks smooth and unmarked on the outside," he said. "But if you look inside you would see a terrible picture. No man can take as much punishment to his head and body as he has over the last twenty years without incurring tremendous damage. I dread to think what might happen if he took a really hard blow to the head. Ali could lose a lot more than a fight. He could lose his health."

In the immediate aftermath of the defeat by Larry Holmes, Ali's friends and family were very concerned about his physical condition and urged him to seek further medical help. Four days after leaving the ring, he finally agreed to go to UCLA Medical Center, where he was taken in for "diagnostic studies" and declared to be in satisfactory condition. It was there that he came under the care of Dr. Dennis Cope in the Division of Endocrinology. It was Cope who unraveled the story of him being over-prescribed and taking an excess of Thyrolar, the thyroid medication, before the bout.

The hospital announced that the patient had suffered "no residual damage" from the beating he took at Holmes's hands, and Ali held a press conference when he was discharged. He explained that he'd only gone to UCLA in the first place "to stop rumors about me being hurt— brain damaged or kidney damaged."

The tragic irony is that as Ali was speaking to the press there was a terrible reminder of the dangers of the sport across town at the California Hospital Medical Center. There, the parents of Johnny Owen, the Welsh bantamweight known as "The Merthyr Matchstick," were keeping vigil at the bedside of their twenty-four-year-old son. Owen had been knocked out in the twelfth round of a bruising World Boxing Council title fight against Mexican champion Lupe Pintor on September 19. He never regained consciousness and died on November 4, forty-six days after being carried from the ring.

Notwithstanding that horrific drama playing out in the city where he now lived, Ali plowed on with his plans to keep fighting, even as his medical problems proliferated over the ensuing months.

On Saturday, June 27, 1981, Ali was scheduled to serve as Grand Marshal in Chicago's New World Patriotism parade along Michigan Avenue. At 8:00 p.m. the night before, he checked into the city's Provident Hospital, complaining of fatigue and weakness.

"I had been after him for months to get a checkup," said his wife Veronica. "He had been coughing for quite some time."

He was admitted immediately, and tests over the course of the weekend established he had walking pneumonia. Or, as he put it himself, he had lung congestion caused by "so much traveling from city to city, country to country, not refusing to talk to anyone."

In any case, he missed the parade, and conscious of the negative headlines spawned by the news he was back in hospital, he commandeered one of the Provident's meeting rooms for a press conference on that Monday. Determined to allay growing public concerns about his health, he rose from his bed, put on a suit and tie, and took the elevator downstairs to the lobby. When he walked in to meet the press, the thrum of the air conditioner was the first thing he noticed.

"Shut off that thing," said Ali. "I don't want double pneumonia!"

Cue laughter. He started off by claiming this had been the longest he'd rested in ten years, and explained why he was there.

"I'm in top-notch shape. But for the past two weeks I've been getting tired and sleepy. I came into the hospital to check it out. They told me I had walking pneumonia."

Having recited his by now-familiar litany of excuses for his failure to perform against Holmes in Vegas, he protested yet again that that wasn't the real him and unveiled a ludicrous plan. He wanted to put together a night of exhibition boxing in which he'd fight two rounds each against Larry Holmes, Gerry Cooney, and Mike Weaver (then the WBA heavyweight champion), just to see if he still had it. Should that evening (he proposed Madison Square Garden as a likely venue) persuade him otherwise, he assured his audience he'd be willing to sign a piece of paper guaranteeing he wouldn't fight again. Of course, he didn't believe it would come to that.

"Life starts at forty and I have the body of a thirty-two-year-old. You thought you'd come here today and see a sick, fat man in a robe, and say, 'I remember when he was something.' Well, don't I look good? I want to be an example for all the people left for dead. What better time to rise up than when people think I'm through, washed up? I want all the people who are left for dead to rise up with me."

To his credit, he appeared tuned in to what was happening in the wider world. "I see those boys starving themselves in Ireland," he said, referencing the Irish Republican prisoners who were then on hunger strike (four had already died), protesting the conditions in the Maze Prison in Northern Ireland. "That's an inspiration to me."

On the way back to the elevator to head up to his room there was the typical Ali crowd scene and kerfuffle. Besieged by nurses asking him to pose for photographs, the more brazen among them even getting kisses, he seemed invigorated by all the attention. He stopped to take a fresh-baked cookie off a tinfoil-covered tray and began to nibble it. And when an elderly patient said, "You're Cassius Clay!" he mock-glared at the man, feigning anger before asking, "You been on the moon?"

Two weeks later, he made good on a promise delivered to the Chicago media by turning up at Deer Lake, his Pennsylvania training camp, and announcing his intention to work on his fitness. The problem was that the tests in Chicago had revealed that his sputum was positive for tuberculosis. This prompted a return to the hospital at UCLA in August, where further tests came back negative for tuberculosis. If the undermining of the earlier diagnosis was a good thing, the doctors in California still found a different reason to be concerned.

"It was on this admission that the people at UCLA began to notice slurred speech," said Dr. Stanley Fahn. "He was examined by a neurologist, who found mild imbalance on walking quickly, but the rest of his examination was normal."

During what was proving to be a summer of medical discontent, Ali had, in the meantime, enlisted the help of another physician. Dr. Harry Demopoulos was a pathologist and an associate professor at New York University Medical Center. The pair had met through a mutual friend, the actor Clint Eastwood, who started working with Demopoulos when he heard about him using vitamins and amino acids to slow down aging.

In July 1981, between his stints in Provident Hospital and UCLA, Ali underwent a battery of tests at NYU during which Demopoulos, shocked at how flabby and out of shape the fighter was, encouraged him to eat better and to try to get back in shape. Not, Demopoulos would later claim, in order to fight again, but just for the good of his health.

This last point is important, because on December 7, Demopoulos arrived in Nassau and started to speak more like a promoter than a physician, offering the press an exceedingly positive take on Ali's health. Indeed, he seemed to be presenting an often bizarre medical validation for the various justifications Ali had cited for wanting to continue.

"There is no damage to any vital organ or system," he said. "Not only was there no evidence of damage, but the physicians were surprised by the positive things we found. We discovered that Muhammad's blood vessels were those of a young man. If you didn't look at the number thirty-nine in the age slot, there is no way you could tell. He's in excellent condition for any activity, and that includes fighting. I do not mean just for this fight. I mean for years to come."

If that optimism startled and scared many long-time Ali watchers, Demopoulos also offered a very strange take on the speech concerns.

"The slurring is real; it is there. But if you examine fighters who are what we call 'punchy,' you will find it is there all the time. With Muhammad, it comes and goes. He came into my class and talked to the med students about the meaning of life, with great wit and conviction. His slurring of speech is more like a valedictorian flubbing his speech, stuttering and stammering from nervousness. It is a psychosocial response from fatigue, from boredom. I have seen it come and go, depending on who he was talking to. The neurologists say they don't need sophisticated equipment to measure punchiness; they just listen. They said Ali is not punchy."

When one reporter put it to Demopoulos that all athletes lose sharpness as they age, and that Ali, closing in on forty, was a prime example, the doctor dismissed the charge.

"Maybe in some athletes. But look at the red-belt karate experts in Japan. They go on until they're fifty and sixty, beating men who are twenty-one. We have an old President who has the toughest job in the world. He was shot badly and nobody said, 'Mr. President, you haven't recovered from the wound.' He did. Look at conductors who lead orchestras at the age of seventy or eighty. Some people are unique."

Demopoulos was speaking with Ali standing next to him, and, on hearing the word unique, the boxer smiled and pointed his index finger at his own head, to remind everybody he was, indeed, special.

For all the doctor's gung-ho talk, though, the testing at NYU had actually uncovered a very serious problem. Ali's CAT scan revealed that, among other damage, his brain had a *cavum septum pellucidum* and an enlarged third ventricle. These were only diagnosed two years after the fact, when *Sports Illustrated* magazine had a neurologist named Dr. Ira Casson re-examine the X-rays for a major feature it ran about boxing and brain damage.

"In the radiologist's written report, these two findings are noted, but the conclusion is that the scan is 'negative', meaning normal," wrote Robert H. Boyle. "It's a question of interpretation. In reviewing CAT scans of the general population, neuroradiologists occasionally see a cavum or a widened third ventricle. This atrophy is more often characteristic of older people. But most neuroradiologists aren't familiar with the scans of boxers. They don't know that the atrophy like that found on Ali's scan shows up in 50 percent of boxers with more than 20 bouts—a percentage far higher than in the general population, and that, by other criteria, these same boxers often show evidence of brain impairment. The cavum abnormality is found four times as frequently in boxers as in non-boxers."

That and other stunning revelations about Ali's physical deterioration remained in the future. In December 1981, he continued to defend his right to fight and reminded critics, "Only Allah knows about my brain!"

Still, conscious of the fact that a growing number of people wanted the Berbick fight not to go ahead for medical reasons, the promoters tried to offer further medical evidence supporting Ali's right to box on. Along with accreditation, journalists arriving to cover the bout were handed a press kit ("Welcome to the biggest card of world-class boxing in history!") that included the medical report conducted by Dr. Dennis Cope at the Division of Endocrinology at UCLA after the Holmes fight.

The report was accompanied by the following note from James Cornelius, President of Sports Internationale Bahamas Ltd. The misspellings didn't do much to enhance the credibility of the angle he was trying to play.

"The following comprehensive medical report on Muhammad Ali was issued by renowned and respected doctors at UCLA," wrote Cornelius. "This concise and conclusive statement erases many doubts and much that is nebulus [sic] and speculative. Lest you fail to read it in its entirety [sic], may I please inform you that it concludes: 'The patient's current health status is excellent and there is no evidence from a health standpoint that he should be limited in his activities.'"

It says something about the nature of the whole event that in an effort to try to convince doubters the promoters took it upon themselves to release a private medical file on a fighter. That the report, which included such details as the fact that Ali had suffered a substantial loss of smell, was dated December 1, 1980, and was already a year out of date, didn't lend much credence to the gambit either.

"The patient tended to talk softly," wrote Cope, "and to almost mumble his speech at times; but when he was questioned about this, he was able to speak appropriately without any evidence of a speech disorder. He was evaluated by a neurosurgeon and neurologist who felt that his speech pattern was not pathologic."

As a public relations maneuver, it was weakened further when Mark Heisler of the *Los Angeles Times* tracked down Dr. Cope, whom Ali had taken to calling "my white doctor."

"This is not an endorsement for him to fight," said Cope. "I never suggested to him that he fight. Basically, this report says that he has no health problems at his time. I'm not saying because of that he should enter into a heavyweight fight. There is no evidence of kidney or liver damage. He was okay for very vigorous activity, like jogging. But that's a bit different from getting in the ring with someone.

"It bothers me that I'm being painted as endorsing him to fight. I cannot go on record saying I endorse Ali fighting again. Ali is in good health. But it becomes another issue at which point an athlete should stop competing in an extremely strenuous sport. I certainly wouldn't want to endorse him fighting."

Cope openly admitted the reflex testing conducted at UCLA was rather crude and couldn't gauge his preparedness to trade punches in a boxing ring. He also pointed out that, since a year had now elapsed since the examination, a more up-to-date medical was in order. When Heisler asked Cope if he had explicitly told Ali not to fight again, he didn't answer. "I consider that kind of question in the area of confidentiality and I intend to talk to Ali about it."

Of course, confidentiality had not seemed to be such an issue when Cornelius was handing out dozens of copies of Cope's investigation of Ali's health, presumably with Ali's permission, throughout the buildup. As the fight drew nearer and nearer, journalists weren't the only ones openly questioning the wisdom of the enterprise.

"He's making a drastic mistake," said Ali's brother Rahaman. "He can get hurt. Look at his body. It's not as solid as it should be. I feel Muhammad is underestimating Berbick, and he can get hurt. He's fought since 1960, and I felt it was time to retire after the second Spinks fight [in November 1978].

"I was against this from the start. That's why I excluded myself from the entourage. I pray to God that my brother comes out of this fight physically and mentally all right. Going into his fortieth year there are dangers, physically, that he faces in this fight. My brother is only human. His flesh and blood is like everyone else's, and his body can only take so much."

His mother, Odessa Clay, made an appearance during one of his sessions at Le Cabaret, bringing a lady backstage to meet her son so he could wish her a happy birthday—the usual cameo of Ali giving somebody a lifelong memory. Yet, when somebody asked Mrs. Clay her opinion of the contest, she spoke from the heart. Like only a mother can.

"I don't think my son should be fighting anymore," said Odessa Clay, "And he knows it. I worry about my son. I worry about him getting seriously hurt. I worry about the punches he takes. His whole family worries about him. My son's almost forty years old now, and that's too old for him to be fighting."

She was asked who, if anybody, had the power to stop her son from boxing.

"Himself," she said. "I just wish my son would realize there comes an age when you should begin taking it easy, even if you're Muhammad Ali."

After one newspaper report carried a quote from eleven-year-old Jamillah Ali, "I'm worried that my daddy might get hurt," the fighter dismissed the idea that many members of his family didn't want him to fight.

"My mother's not worried," said Ali. "My wife's not worried. None of my children are worried. My father keeps pushing me."

His father wasn't pushing him but, having been highly critical of the decision to fight Holmes the previous year, Cassius Clay Sr. was a lot more stoic this time around.

"My son has told me he wants to continue fighting because he loves the publicity," said Clay Sr. "You know, he don't wanna die, he loves the public, loves crowds. Ring-wise, I think my son can take care of himself. He's over twenty-one, isn't he? So I'm certainly not gonna stop him."

Eight days before Ali was due to step into the ring, Joe Frazier made his own comeback on a night that should have set alarm bells off in Nassau. In a half-empty amphitheater hard by the stockyards on the south side of Chicago, with a tell-tale paunch where his washboard stomach used to be, Frazier endured the all-too-familiar ending to every boxing tale, the usual poignant finale: long on guts, short on glamour and glory.

"We don't want a requiem for a heavyweight played on NBC," said Dr. Ferdie Pacheco, explaining why the network where he was employed as a commentator had, like all others, refused to show the fight. This wasn't a contest anybody needed or wanted, except one stubborn old bruiser from Philadelphia who, sixteen years on from his professional debut, reckoned his infamous left hook was immune to the ravages of aging.

"The networks didn't want us," said Frazier about the mainstream television channels' lack of interest in bouts involving him and Ali. "Two old black brothers trying to come back, must have partied all their money away."

In a softening of the long-standing enmity between the pair, he even received a phone call from his nemesis just after he weighed in at 220 pounds.

"We got to make the old men proud," said Ali.

"I hear you," said Frazier. "I'm gonna hold my end of the deal up."

"We're old men and we gotta show the world we can do it."

"Don't call me old," said Frazier.

On December 3, six years after Eddie Futch famously stopped the Thrilla in Manila by whispering in his ear, "No one will ever forget what you did here today," Frazier went ten mediocre rounds with Floyd "Jumbo" Cummings. More than five years since George Foreman battered Frazier into retirement at Nassau Coliseum, he'd returned to the ring one more time, so far off-Broadway as to be almost forgotten.

His purse was $80,000, a substantial sum even if it was less than his training expenses used to be for the marquee fights of his heyday, those epics that made him forever part of fistic folklore. At this point in his life, Frazier's pension was reportedly paying him $70,000 a year, but he had extensive interests in businesses that weren't exactly flourishing.

"I always need money," said Frazier. "I love to spend money. I love to party. I have the ability, the energy, the know-how. Why take all that energy and know-how and party with it? Why waste it?"

Cummings had turned pro at twenty-nine after serving twelve years for murder in Stateville Correctional Center in Illinois, a menacing biographical detail that always helped the box office. With the muscle-bound upper body of a man who'd pumped a lot of iron in the prison yard, he lacked the skills of a genuine contender and, at least in this contest, tired way too easily. Twice in the eighth round, however, he pinned Frazier to the ropes and pounded him with flurries of unanswered punches. It was the sort of cameo many feared Berbick would soon be visiting on Ali in Nassau.

Had it been anybody else other than Frazier's twenty-one-year-old son Marvis working his corner that night, a towel might have been thrown in and the suffering ended. But Futch had refused to get involved in this particular charade because he knew too well how the story would end.

Perhaps buoyed by voices in the crowd sporadically calling out for "Smokin," Frazier stayed upright for two more rounds, the last vestiges of his stubborn self. Cummings had done more than enough to win, but two myopic judges declared it a draw. What the press recognized as a sympathy vote, an attempt to spare an icon further embarrassment, Frazier interpreted as a sort of supernatural vindication.

"I'm one of God's men," he said afterwards. "Separate me from the rest of them. Things that happen to me don't happen to every man."

That night, Frazier sat in his hotel room surrounded by brown paper bags of freshly-delivered pizza and cartons of orange juice. A once star-studded entourage had shrunk to just him and his immediate family. His face was freshly nicked and puffed up where he'd taken too many punches, one eye still leaking blood, enough physical evidence to betray a tough night at the office.

When reporters arrived, he claimed to be celebrating the first draw of his career and talked defiantly of plans to wrest control of the heavyweight division from Larry Holmes. Nobody does delusion quite like a boxer pretending not to have heard the final bell.

"I feel sorry for people who think they're growing old," said Frazier. "I've got a mother who's seventy-two and she's stronger than me and you. I don't know nothin' about growing old. You've got to have positive thinking. You can't get old and die at thirty-eight."

Does he feel at all like a shadow of his former self?

"Your shadow is you," said Frazier animatedly. "You can't separate that. Your shadow is with you everywhere you go. Late in the day it just gets longer."

Although Frazier was talking up his desire to box again by March—something nobody else who witnessed him stealing a draw against Cummings had any desire to see—Illinois boxing officials were already saying they would not allow him to fight in their state again.

More pertinent yet, George Vecsey, in Chicago to cover Frazier for the *New York Times* before heading to the Bahamas, reckoned what he'd just witnessed should serve as a warning for Ali and his handlers.

"Jeremiah Shabazz, a Muslim minister [who'd been close to Ali since he first joined the Nation of Islam], flew up from Nassau to watch the other half of The Odd Couple," wrote Vecsey. "Mr. Shabazz reports that Ali has been looking better since Angelo Dundee arrived last week, and that the rolls around Ali's waist have been trimmed somewhat. But Mr. Shabazz saw Joe Frazier, covering up in a corner, taking shots from Jumbo Cummings. If he is truly a friend of Ali, he will tell him honestly just how bad Frazier looked. There is still time for Muhammad Ali to save his health and his dignity."

CHAPTER SEVEN
If You Build It...

It's important to get out with the title, with the briefcase, with the necktie. Look at Pelé, he's getting out of soccer now while people remember the best. He came over to see me at my hotel. He invited me to his last game. He got to me. I was going to get to him, but he got to me first. But he's right. It's important for people to remember the best.
Muhammad Ali, New York, October 1, 1977

FROM THE MOMENT HE STARTED to dream of putting together a Muhammad Ali fight in the early part of 1981, the specter of Don King had hung over James Cornelius. Before any contracts were signed, he was constantly worried about the most experienced and infamous promoter in America using his long-standing relationship with Ali to push him out of the way. Of course, when the wheels started to come off and the money to dry up in November, and Ali asked him if he'd be willing to walk away for a cash payment, Cornelius saw the hand of King in the offer.

It turns out his paranoia was well-founded, even if his sense of direction about it was slightly askew.

On Saturday, December 5, King arrived in Freeport, the Bahamian island where Berbick had been finishing his own preparations for the fight. Unsurprisingly, given the frequency with which Berbick switched promoters, King claimed he had a previous option on him dating back to his defeat by Larry Holmes.

"Mr. Berbick had agreed at that time to have Don King Productions promote his next fight," said King. "Despite this agreement, Mr. Berbick then signed a contract with James Cornelius of Sports Internationale to fight Muhammad Ali. After breaking our contract, Berbick came to my office in New York and pleaded with me not to object to his participation in the Ali fight. They're going to have to pay me some money if they are going to put on that fight."

Whether King wanted $200,000 or $100,000 to go away depends on who you believe, but he definitely wasn't going to settle for anything less than six figures. It was a hefty sum to be looking for on any given day, but especially at a time when all around this beleaguered bout cash was in increasingly short supply.

When he heard what was afoot, Cornelius chartered a plane from Nassau (an expensive move for a financially-strapped outfit), made the short hop across to Freeport, and went immediately to the Bahamas Princess Hotel, where both Berbick and now King were billeted. In his version of the story, Cornelius was accompanied by one man, somebody he referred to as his guard and whose only function was to escort King's lawyer Charles Lomax outside the room while the two men negotiated.

"Within a few seconds, he finished his telephone conversation and, to my surprise, sprang from the bed and grabbed me by the collar, pressing me hard for $100,000," wrote Cornelius. "Then everything went black. I could only remember blood running from his mouth like an open faucet, which had apparently drenched my shirt."

The fighting over, Cornelius then claims to have warned King to pack his suitcase and make ready to leave the island immediately. Indeed, he even escorted him downstairs to the taxi that took him to the airport. Nothing personal, just business.

King's account of what happened in the hotel room as he was getting dressed that Sunday morning is different and a lot more menacing. By his reckoning, Cornelius came to the door equipped for trouble, and flanked by four heavies from the Nation of Islam who quickly set upon him.

"Four of them were beating me up," King later told the FBI. "But as they were working me over, I got two of them, named Omar and Luke, on the side. I slipped them two hundred dollars each and asked them to take it easy on me, not to kick me so hard. Right away, Omar told Cornelius, 'I think we done enough,' and I knew my money was working for me already."

As King lay there bleeding from his wounds, Cornelius warned him to go back to America or the next beating he'd receive would be fatal.

Although the details of their memories don't quite coalesce, all agree King left Freeport in a hurry. He flew to Fort Lauderdale, where he ended up being treated at Broward County Medical Center for head and face wounds. Amid reports of him losing teeth and suffering a broken nose, speculation began that he might require plastic surgery. Meanwhile, eyewitnesses to the fracas were in short supply.

"I didn't know Don was down here until Cornelius called me Saturday night," said Berbick's trainer, Lee Black. "Don had some papers he had to give me for the Saoul Mamby fight in Nigeria. I saw Don briefly on Sunday morning, and the next I heard he had this trouble. He told me Cornelius and three other guys did it."

Berbick also claimed to be completely out of the loop.

"I just saw Don briefly in the dining room while he delivered some material to my manager," said Berbick, perhaps wisely staying above the fray. "I don't know anything else."

At least that's what he said in public. In private, he was shocked at how one of the most feared and powerful men in boxing had been run out of town.

"Man, this is one hell of a place," he told Fred Sturrup, a local journalist. "I thought you guys were small time. Man, Don King came in and he thought he had his program together. He wanted to do his thing but look what happened to him. You people don't fool around in this place. I just want to go to Nassau and fight Ali and get out of here."

After King's press agent in New York released a statement accusing him of this vicious assault, Cornelius was forced to respond with an emphatic and completely false denial of involvement. At first, he couldn't be found to issue a statement. Eventually, the press pack tracked him down to a pool hall and bar called the Zanzibar Club, where he claimed this was the first he'd heard of the attack. Apparently, he'd been too busy working on the fight to read the paper.

"That's bull! I don't know anything about it," said Cornelius. "I haven't even talked to Don King. I know nothing about it at all."

That King was badly injured can be gauged from the fact that later in the week he had to do something unthinkable for him, canceling a press conference scheduled to announce the forthcoming Wilfred Benitez–Roberto Duran fight. He didn't stop yapping to reporters in private, though, telling one he had personally informed Alfred Maycock, the Bahamian Minister of Economic Planning, about the assault, and he'd been assured by the Nassau government that the assailants would be arrested and punished for the crime.

They never were and were never likely to be, given that Cornelius had discussed King's financial demands with Kendal Nottage, the Minister for Youth and Culture, even before flying to Freeport to meet King and deliver payment of a different kind.

Meanwhile, when reporters back in Nassau informed Ali that five mysterious men had given King a beating, quick as a flash he asked, "Was one of them Berbick?" And, perhaps because so many of those present knew how many fighters, including Ali himself, had been ripped off by the man with the distinctive hair, the room dissolved in laughter.

* * *

During the October press conference at the Beverly Wilshire Hotel, before Muhammad Ali, Trevor Berbick, and Thomas Hearns took center stage, Shelly Saltman had introduced two businessmen to the audience: Lionel Schaen and John Ettlinger. Neither would have been well-known to most journalists in the room, but they were still given some time at the lectern to publicize their roles. The presence of television executives, even if they weren't representing the mainstream networks, all of whom had passed on the show, meant the fight was going to be broadcast. That, of course, meant the whole promotion now appeared to be on a sounder financial footing.

"The event that is about to take place on December 11th is going to be a very momentous event," said Schaen, President of SelecTV, starting the sales pitch. "Just from the sheer presence in this room of all of you people this morning, it's overwhelming. We've had several press conferences over the past few months to promote the Hearns-Leonard fight, which as you know was one of the biggest grosses of all time, taking in excess of $40 million. The press conferences, both in Los Angeles and New York, for that do not compare with what we have here today.

"This brings us to the event on the 11th. We think that we have one of the finest fight cards in a long time, led by Muhammad Ali and Trevor Berbick, along with Thomas Hearns and Greg Page. We think this is going to be a spectacular event. Sales are going far better than we expected this early, and the requests are coming in from all over the world to broadcast the event."

Schaen had a long track record in the television business since starting out working for ABC in New York. He sounded ebullient and confident that there was a genuine market out there for the contest, despite so many other people believing otherwise. The latter viewpoint was bolstered when he started to explain the rather labyrinthine arrangements that would be in place to bring Ali vs. Berbick to the largest audience possible.

"We are doing something different for this one, something that's never been done before," said Schaen. "The distribution in the United States is going to be done through cable, pay TV and pay per view, along with open system. Some systems will be giving it to subscribers, other systems will be charging a fee to watch it. We expect the event to bring in a gross of between $10 [million] and $15 million."

That sounded like a lot of money for a fight that was generating so little enthusiasm, given the fact that, after the Holmes debacle, most right-thinking boxing fans had no appetite to watch Ali suffer in the ring again. Where did he get the number from?

"The gentlemen to my left and right [Ali, Hearns, and Berbick] are responsible for the great demands being put on us already," he said. "We just started selling this a few days ago, and people are calling in from all over the world for it. I'm very pleased to be part of it, to be associated with Medallion Films, who'll be handling the international part of it."

That was the cue for John Ettlinger, the owner of Medallion Films, to take the podium.

"This is quite a partnership," said Ettlinger, another veteran in the business who'd gotten his start managing a movie theater in New York City after serving in World War II. "It took quite a while to put it to bed; everybody is finally very happy, maybe a little tired. [Smiling.] But it's a very interesting thing because Lionel Schaen and I have been friends for many, many years, and here we find ourselves partnered with SelecTV, and I think this is going to be a great event."

It had taken three weeks for Schaen and Ettlinger to reach agreement on a deal to televise the fight in America and wherever else was interested. They'd first met to discuss the possibility in Los Angeles on October 8, by which time Ettlinger had been offered the opportunity to purchase the telecast rights from Sports Internationale. Both men reckoned there was enough lingering interest in Ali's career for money to made off the fight, and at one of their subsequent meetings Schaen claimed that SelecTV already had $2 million in guaranteed sales in America alone.

Buoyed by this, the pair established a joint venture for the event, calling it Medsel, and they paid just over $2 million for the domestic and worldwide rights. Then they proceeded to talk up the significance of the contest at every turn, helped by Ali who told reporters, "Two billion people will be conscious of my fight."

Which was a little bit of a stretch.

"We're going to set a precedent for the industry with the technological innovations we'll be using," said Schaen on November 24. "The fight will be seen in five million homes in America. Twenty-five million people will watch this."

To deliver the first ever live transmission from the Bahamas, Medsel put together a sixty-man production team with six cameras, four videotape machines, and a graphics generator, in addition to the satellite uplink. They were determined to do everything right, although Schaen wouldn't confirm what satellite was going to be used in order to protect the operation against pirates and bootleggers. He was, however, willing to hype up the event into which he'd sunk so much money.

"Boxing is what it is today because of what it was in the fifties when TV made it a major vehicle," said Schaen. "Cable TV is going to take it even farther. These two are among the most popular fighters of the day. Muhammad Ali is a legend and Thomas Hearns is a top contender. Ali is in as good a shape as he's been in for five years. For his last fight he dropped to 215 pounds and it put him down mentally and physically. He'll weigh in at 230 this time, which is his proper weight. Jersey Joe Walcott won the title at thirty-nine, Jim Fitzsimons was forty-five [sic]. Archie Moore was forty-two when he was light-heavyweight champ. Ali has all the money he needs. Ego is it. He wants to be before the public again. He just feeds off that."

By late November, Schaen was standing by his contention that the total gross would be somewhere between $10 million and $15 million even though sales had, in reality, been disappointing. Seriously disappointing. For all the attempts to hype up the event, the interest in Ali just wasn't there anymore. There was a reason the main networks and HBO had passed on the opportunity to show the fight. They didn't want to be associated with a contest of dubious merit that everybody suspected might involve the most beloved fighter of the age being embarrassed and/or hurt.

While Schaen and Ettlinger's joint venture would end up wending its way through the courts for five years after the event, the fact is that, despite the lack of commercial interest, just pulling off a broadcast from Nassau at that time turned out to be quite a technical feat.

"My company, Satellite Sports, which I owned with Beverly Hills lawyer Phil Gillen, was engaged to handle worldwide marketing, the staging of the event, and production of the TV program," said Shelly

Saltman. "It was the most bizarre major fight I have ever been involved in, Two days before, our satellite dish, which we were shipping in from Tampa, Florida by barge, was lost in a storm when the barge overturned. It was recovered weeks after the fight was over.

"The brilliant Clair Higgins, the man who invented the TV mobile unit, he was in charge of production. He had a microwave link set up flown in, and at the same time he had one set up on the roof of Tampa's tallest hotel in order that by line of sight we could get out a signal. This signal was then uplifted to the satellite from the roof, and the on-air show was on."

If Saltman's official title was co-owner and president of Satellite Sports, he touched down in Nassau in mid-November trailing quite the reputation as a heavy hitter. Between Cleveland, New York, and Los Angeles, his career in sports and entertainment promotion and publicity had seen him work with such luminaries as Jack Benny, Jackie Gleason, and Andy Williams in their prime.

While he'd been involved in the epic Ali-Frazier trilogy, Saltman also had some curious entries on his resume. Evel Knievel's ill-fated attempt to jump the Snake River Canyon in Idaho in 1974 was an unfortunate episode that culminated in the daredevil later seriously assaulting Saltman with a baseball bat. He'd also been responsible for Ali's ridiculous and ultimately demeaning hybrid bout with the Japanese wrestler Antonio Inoki at the Nippon Budokan in Tokyo in 1976.

Saltman was close enough to Ali, though, to consider him a friend. Indeed, he was one of those in the dressing room holding ice to his broken jaw in the aftermath of his defeat by Norton in their first meeting, back in 1973. He arrived in the Bahamas determined to put together a first-class production, knowing that this might well be Ali's last dance. In this regard, the scale of the task facing him hit home when he made his first reconnaissance trip to check out the Queen Elizabeth Sports Center: a site regal by name, not by nature.

"Wow!" said Saltman. "What a shock! It was a large open field with a broken down wooden fence partially surrounding it, that and a hut that was supposedly a box office, and virtually nothing else. Here, in three weeks, we were expected to put on a major televised sports event."

Saltman's stunned verdict was in keeping with the response of just about every other newcomer to the island when they first set eyes on the place that was going to host Ali's sixty-first bout.

Here was the take of veteran boxing scribe Tom Cushman:

"Although the facility was called the Queen Elizabeth Stadium, the queen undoubtedly would prefer to discard any association with it," wrote Cushman. "Part of a landing field for bombers during World War II, it appeared to have taken several direct hits. The reason for my visit was to scout working-press arrangements. Over the years, one learns to do this so as not to be too unpleasantly surprised when the work night arrives. Not only was there no press seating at QES that day, there was no seating for anyone."

It was Saltman's job to ensure that seats were found. And quickly. Some bleachers were commandeered from local high schools. As many folding chairs as could be sourced were borrowed from hotels, most of which gave them free in the spirit of goodwill and in the hope of assisting the hosting of an event they felt was good for tourism on the island. If the scale of the production was much bigger than anybody on the ground was used to, the biggest problem was that the scarcity of money ensured workers were not being paid on time.

Melvin Pace was foreman of the crew charged with setting up the stadium. Aside from letting slip that the initial order to locate 17,000 chairs had been drastically reduced to 11,000—from an initial design of twenty-seven rows of bleachers, there would be just twelve by fight time—he also told reporters spectators were fortunate they'd have some place to sit at all. With just days to go until the first bell, Pace and his colleagues were so irate about not receiving the wages due that they came within an hour of walking off the job altogether and leaving town. Another crisis was averted. Just.

The changes to the seating numbers starkly illustrated just how badly the fight was selling. Almost from the moment the promotion had been announced, there had, typically, been an attempt by some of those involved to exaggerate the market for tickets. As early as October 30, Franklyn Wilson, a Bahamian accountant now being described as vice-president of Sports Internationale, was claiming from Nassau that four hundred VIP seats had already been sold for $1,000 each and the public were going to snap up the $50 passes.

"Everything is going very well," said Wilson. "Tour operators are organizing large groups to come down for the weekend. We hope to add a gala musical extravaganza. We'll be announcing our worldwide television plans very soon. Seats are being added to the stadium now."

That was weeks before a single seat was put in place; the VIPs would end up sitting in steel bridge chairs. Then again, exaggeration quickly became the norm when discussing the logistics of this event. By November 25, just 2,000 tickets in total had been sold and James Cornelius went on the offensive, claiming this was no big deal because they expected 70 to 80 percent of the gate to turn up to pay on the night of the fight. If they were expecting that type of last-minute turn-out, their next move was ludicrous.

By the time December rolled around, the $50 tickets, the cheapest on offer, were reduced to $10 in supermarkets all over Nassau, and visiting journalists found butchers' shops flogging them for half that sum. The *Nassau Guardian* ran a cartoon on December 4 depicting Cornelius holding somebody labeled "Bahamian Fight Fan" by the ankles and shaking him down for money.

"Come on…you know you wan' see der fight!" says the Cornelius character.

"What make yinna tink 'bout us all of a sudden?" asks the upside-down local.

Even if the Bahamian papers were now mocking him, Cornelius tried to put on a brave face.

"We've sold 5,000 tickets; they are going very, very fast," he said, four days before the fight.

Meanwhile, Saltman had other concerns, such as finding a lighting rig, communications facilities, and power sources for a fight scheduled to take place after dark. The initial signs were not good. None of the usual heavy equipment was on hand or, indeed, anyplace around the island. The local companies wanted to help, and the national government was determined to assist in any way they could. The problem was that almost everything to produce a modern telecast had to be imported from Florida.

Saltman didn't stint when it came to putting together the team to call the fight.

"As blow-by-blow commentator, I had the great Don Dunphy, my mentor, and boxing's foremost Hall-of-Fame announcer. Doing color, I had referee Davey Pearl, who was the third man in the ring for the first Leonard-Hearns fight three months earlier. In addition, I had Randy Shields, often called the uncrowned welterweight, and the only man to ever beat Leonard in the amateurs also doing color. Plus, I introduced CBS's Jim Hill in his first ever role as MC of a major event."

On the morning of the fight, Saltman and Higgins got to the stadium early to go over the arrangements. Some of the ringside seating and furniture needed to be moved to make space for equipment. While re-arranging the VIP section, the local police spotted them loitering by the chairs reserved for Prime Minister Lynden O. Pindling and his entourage, and decided they were up to no good. Within minutes, they were on their way downtown to jail.

"Ever been in a Bahamian jail?" remembered Saltman. "It was filthy and in need of a good washing. It reeked of urine and there was only a small window for the light to shine through. It was around 10:00 a.m. in the morning when they tossed us in a cell, and we were told everyone on the island was busy with the fight, so we would not be arraigned until the following day when they could get a judge."

There Saltman and Higgins would most likely have stayed, except that Randy Shields had spotted them being frog-marched away by police and told Phil Gillen. It took a couple of hours for Gillen to convince the authorities that the pair were simply working the fight, not plotting to assassinate the head of state. Just after midday, they were back at the Queen Elizabeth Arena trying to put everything in place for the fight to go ahead.

And there was still plenty to do.

Patti Dreifuss, a veteran publicist in the boxing world with credits including the Thrilla in Manila, had been hired to coordinate the press coverage in the stadium. Having been shown a map of the arena layout that boasted 204 media spaces necklaced around the ring, she discovered that the reality of the situation on the ground was, like so much with this fight, very different. Upon walking into the Queen Elizabeth Sports Center, she found just forty spaces. And then there was the matter of telephones. Or the lack thereof.

Initial press concerns about the difficulty of phoning newspaper offices across America from ringside had been assuaged by a representative of Batelco, the Bahamian telephone company. When reporters inquired as to whether they'd have to pay any money to secure the service, they were assured that wouldn't be necessary. Then, as the fight drew nearer, they discovered that only sixteen phones could be set up in the stadium, and that each of those would require a hefty financial deposit. Moreover, the company would not be taking credit cards—just cold, hard cash.

On fight night, the press ending up having to clamber over a three-and-a-half-foot high cement wall just to get to their seats. When they got there, they discovered workmen from the telephone company still scrambling around to put lines in place even as the first boxers on the undercard were being shepherded into the arena.

CHAPTER EIGHT
Trouble in Paradise Island

One more fight, that's all. Then I'll retire.

Muhammad Ali, New York City, May 23, 1978

FIVE DAYS BEFORE THE FIGHT, Angelo Dundee was in Hollywood, Florida, at the baseball winter meetings. It was a measure of the profile he'd gained through his lengthy association with Muhammad Ali that he was there to promote a sportswear company with which he had a commercial relationship. Inevitably, one of the journalists monitoring baseball trades got around to talking boxing and asked about whether Ali had enough left to defeat Trevor Berbick.

"I've never been more convinced of anything in my life," said Dundee. "I didn't want Ali to take another fight, but he was determined. He wants to wipe out the memory in the public's eye of his terrible performance against Larry Holmes."

When Dundee arrived at the Britannia Beach Hotel on Tuesday afternoon, December 8, he found Ali holding court in room 642, lounging on his bed in a robe, surrounded by reporters, opining on everything from Holy War to holes in Berbick's defenses. Same tableau as it ever was. The two men hugged like the old friends they were. But, of course, many of those present knew one of them was actually a lot more enthusiastic about Friday night's forthcoming festivities than the other.

"Angelo thinks I shouldn't be fightin'," said Ali earlier in the week. "He's coming in to work the corner but he thinks I'm shot, my legs have gone. But Angelo's not me. He don't know what I've got."

Dundee did his best to dispel any idea he might have sat this one out, telling those witnessing the reunion, "If he's determined to fight, I'll be in his corner."

At which point Ali started to boast anew about how well his sparring had been going during his celebrated trainer's absence, citing in particular an uplifting encounter with the next biggest name on the fight card.

"I had a four-round brawl with Hearns, and it was right on," said Ali.

"With Tommy?" Dundee asked.

"Stickin' and jabbin'. Over his jab. Trading punches. Getting him in the corners. One on one."

"I love you going with little guys," said Dundee. "I love it."

Ali had indeed sparred with Hearns, and afterwards the Detroit fighter reckoned there could be only one winner of the main event.

"Ali can still do anything with the left hand that he wants," said Hearns. "I think he's a much better man than Berbick. I had the pleasure of seeing Berbick fight before and he don't have the style of Ali. He's not of the caliber of Ali. I feel that with Ali's ability that he can go on and be victorious."

Hearns was standing by his man, but others who witnessed their spar remember it differently, recalling an embarrassing affair in which the gulf between the elderly (at least in boxing terms) Ali and a young fighter in his prime was all too apparent. Hearns was fast and occasionally furious, dictating the pace and the style of the exercise; Ali was ponderous, one-paced, and restricted mostly to heavy-handed pawing.

"He floated like an anchor and stung like a moth," quipped Tony Segreto of NBC in Miami.

The snippet of surviving video footage shows Ali being bullied around the ring by a thin, rangy man in a yellow singlet in a way that didn't bode well for his chances against a larger opponent bent on really hurting him.

Tellingly though, within twenty-four hours of arriving, Dundee had, at least for public consumption, started singing from Ali's hymn sheet. "I was very pleased with what I saw with the way he is working. To be quite honest, I didn't think he could go through it again. He's ready to beat Berbick."

Whether oblivious or impervious to the logistical mess going on around him, Ali stuck diligently to the task of giving the writers who'd flown in to chronicle his latest escapade the type of gold they'd come to expect from him.

One minute he was talking about his plans to write a book…

"On middle age and me. How to get in shape. What you do every day. For ten weeks. How many rounds on the speed bag."

…the next he was repackaging the contest as a sporting jihad.

"I am a warrior of Islam. This is a Holy War. I am fighting for Allah. I am fighting for my religion, not because I enjoy fighting. People all around the world listen to me and I bring them the word of Allah. Before I won the championship from Liston I used to go to the mosque in Miami in secret. I didn't want the white press to know because I knew they wasn't ready for it. Look at what I've accomplished. People don't think twice about Muslim names. Look at all the ballplayers with Muslim names."

He went from explaining how Berbick would succumb…

"When he gets in the ring and looks at my face, I'll just whisper one word to him, 'pressure.' Meeting me is pressure. That's why he's not here. His people are doing everything to keep him away from me. I'd do anything to see him right in front of me, right now. Just want to look at him. You see, it's so hard to challenge me, because you're actually fighting the powers of the universe."

…to berating those around him for lacking imagination.

"He who has no imagination stands on the earth. Columbus had imagination. The Wright brothers had imagination. The astronauts had imagination. People are worried about me, more worried than when

Evel Knievel was gonna jump the Grand Canyon, more worried than when the astronauts went into space, more worried than when some blind men climbed a mountain. I'm not worried. I'm so happy. I'm only worried that the fight is not gonna come off. I'm worried that Berbick won't show up. I'm worried that he'll get bit by a dog. I'm worried that he might get hurt on the way to the fight."

One question too many about whether the primary reason he was here was financial sparked an angry response. "People always think Negro boxers need money. Do I ask you if you need money? Do you?"

When the reporter didn't answer, somebody blurted out that Berbick hoped to buy a new house with his purse. Enough of a prompt for Ali to explain he needed $1 million for a much higher purpose, to fund his grand plan to embark on a campaign of "Islamic evangelism" all over the planet. Then, he used this as a stick to beat Berbick.

"I'm fighting for my four children. For my mother out there watching, for my wife out there watching, for my father out there watching, for my people. It's a holy war. These are things I'd die for. I'm going into battle, prepared to die. And all he's fighting for is a house?"

At last, he seemed to be working himself up to something approaching disdain for the man he was going to box.

"He's getting more money than when he fought Holmes. He's getting more recognition. He is an amateur. He has no experience. He has no class."

He even admitted that the arrival of so many members of the press had exhilarated him and improved his training.

"The hard part was working for the fight before people knew there was a fight, working when the press weren't writing about it. I trained better today knowing you were here, knowing I'm forty, that I'm not supposed to be doing this. You see, I'm a rebel. Vietnam—I didn't go, joined the Black Muslims at a time when Negroes were scared to walk to Muslim mosques, on the stands with Elijah Muhammad, preaching the doom of America, standing next to the boldest black man ever to hit America.

"Look at the kind of man you're dealing with. Weigh up my life, you won't be surprised by what I do. I'm right there with white people in Georgia and Mississippi, preachin' that Americans lynched, slaved, burned, robbed us. Raped our women. White men ain't no good, never be no good. We were preachin' that stuff. That takes more of a man than to fight Berbick."

While many of the journalists in his orbit that week had been there almost since the beginning, witnessing versions of this long-playing show at his various stops all over the planet, there were newcomers in the pack, too. One neophyte marveled at what Ali was like to deal with.

Stephen Bezanson covered sports for the *Chronicle-Herald* in Halifax. Ushered into Ali's company after one press engagement, he confessed his loyalty to Berbick, the fighter who'd made that Canadian city his home, the reason this reporter was in the Caribbean.

"Muhammad, I've been a fan of yours my whole life, but in this bout I'm cheering for Berbick because he's my meal ticket," said Bezanson.

"Son, if you can't cheer for your hometown boy you're not much of a man," said Ali.

Whatever was going to happen thereafter, he'd left a unique impression.

"I just said to myself, 'Wow, here's this guy who is the most recognized athlete in the world and he doesn't take for a moment what I said personally,'" said Bezanson. "Totally grounded and incredibly humble, despite all that he had accomplished."

Humble and entertaining.

"I still got my hand speed, don't I?" Ali asked another reporter.

"Yes," came the answer.

That simple affirmation wasn't enough. Ali invited him to put his hands up for a demonstration, so he could show that he did, indeed, retain his legendary speed.

"Pop! Pop! Pop!" he shouted, as he peppered each palm. "This is what I'm going to do to Berbick. In and out. Come in and throw a punch and get out. I'll be moving. I'll be dancing. I'll shock the world. I'll show the press who said I was too old to box no more. I'm not too old! I just thought of something. Age is mind over matter. As long as you don't mind, it don't matter. That's pretty good, ain't it?"

It *was* pretty good. In fact, it was pretty good the first time Mark Twain, to whom the quote is usually attributed, came up with it nearly a century earlier.

No matter how lackluster his workouts, no matter how worrying his physical condition, his charm remained intact. One afternoon, he was asked to head into town to shoot a promotional film to be broadcast before the fight. The limousine ferrying him around pulled up at a fish market where, of course, he was besieged by well-wishers and autograph hunters. He humored them one and all, the smile, the joshing, the charisma that had wowed fans of every nationality for two decades on full display.

"I love people," said Ali after climbing back into the car, leaning back in the seat, satisfied at this particular part of his job done well. Again.

Crucially, and in the way that perhaps separated him from so many other athletes in the spotlight, he was as ebullient when the camera was off as when it was on. The enthusiasm was never faked. At the end of one session with the press, he announced that he was shutting it down for the remainder of the week, cutting himself off from everybody to prepare for the battle ahead.

"I'm going to rest after this until the fight itself," he said. "I'm going to my apartment and going to be by myself. No press, no visitors. That's it."

Within the hour, Veronica Ali had met a group of five schoolgirls whose greatest wish was to meet the boxer who was the talk of the island they called home. The ban on public engagements was quickly lifted and the quintet was granted an audience with a smile. Each received a kiss on the cheek and then, because he couldn't help himself, he started doing magic tricks. He needed to entertain like he needed oxygen.

Here, even in the dying days of his professional career, few were immune to the Ali magic. There was a reception at the US Embassy

Ali taking punishment from Larry Holmes in Las Vegas in the fight that cost him his license there. (AP)

Ali at the Waldorf–Astoria announcing his comeback. (AP/Marty Lederhandler)

Ali uses his fists to make a point to the press as James Cornelius watches on. (AP)

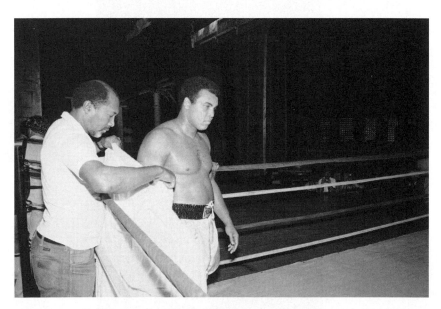

Ali about to begin a workout in the dining room of the Britannia Beach Hotel. (AP/Gene Blythe)

Berbick tucking into a massive lunch on the day of the fight. (AP/Richard Drew)

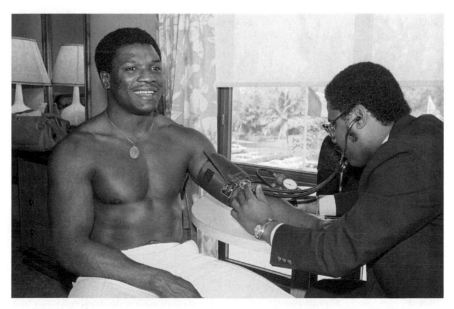

Dr. Perry Gomez putting Berbick through his pre-fight medical. (AP/Richard Drew)

The Louisville Lip staying uncharacteristically quiet at the weigh-in. (AP/Bill Brodrick)

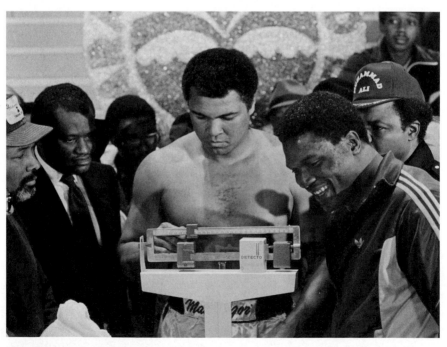

The sight of Ali on the scales makes Trevor Berbick smile. (AP/Phil Sandlin)

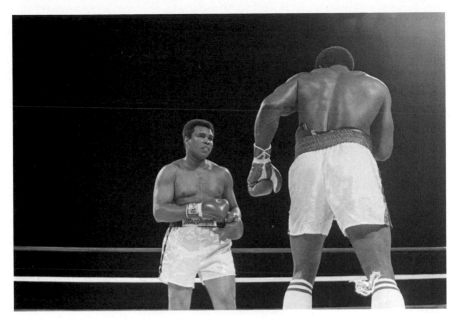

Ali looking ponderous early in the first round. (AP)

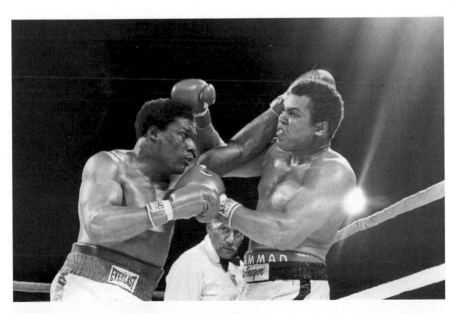

Ali on the ropes, Berbick on the attack. (AP)

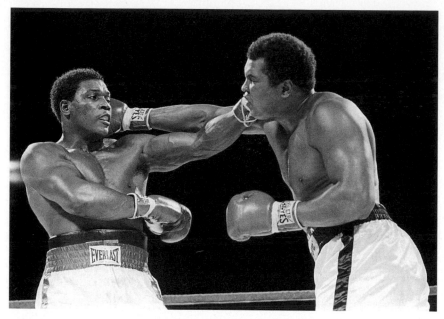

Ali and Berbick go toe to toe. (AP)

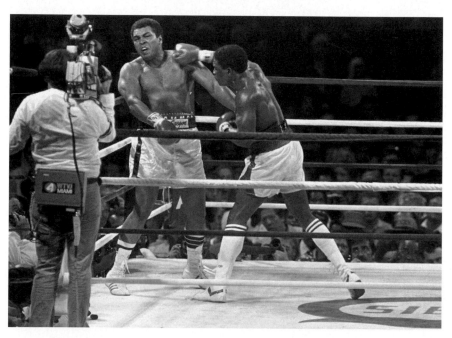

Trevor Berbick connects with a right to Muhammad Ali's head. (AP)

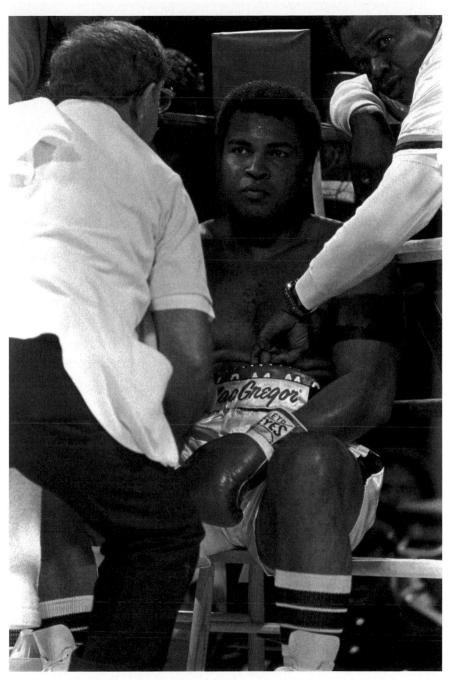

Ali feeling the pace as Angelo Dundee offers advice between rounds. (AP)

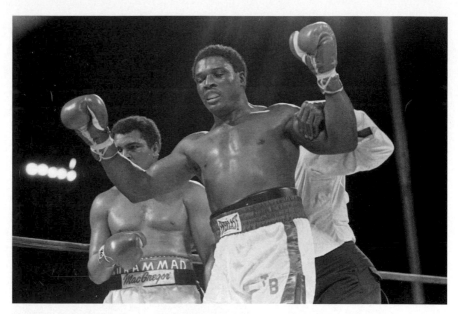

Berbick raises his arms at the sound of the final bell. (AP)

To the victor the spoils. Berbick being carried in triumph. (AP)

where Ali's best friend, Howard Bingham, took a photograph of him yukking it up with Andrew F. Antippas, the US Charge d'Affaires in the Bahamas. Of course, Antippas was also reckoned to be the CIA station chief in the country and was later accused by the government of trying to destabilize it. That would be the same administration that had welcomed the Ali fight as a way of garnering favorable publicity for a still-young nation.

The USS *DuPont* pulled into Nassau during Ali's stay and, with James Cornelius accompanying him, Ali boarded the ship. The most famous conscientious objector in the history of the US Armed Forces was now the esteemed guest of the US Navy.

"As we approached the deck where the crew had been assembled by the top brass, the Commander handed me two naval caps and asked me if the champ could put one on," wrote Cornelius. "I walked over to the microphone where Ali was about to address the men and handed him the cap. He took it and pulled it down over his short crop...Ali looked out at the men and said, 'Ya know, they tried to get me on one of these things once.' The men all laughed. He then said very seriously, 'Fight for your country!' He sparred a few rounds with a couple of men and we departed."

The Bahamian politicians wrung him for every drop of positive publicity they could manage, too. His visit to Kendal Nottage at the Ministry for Youth, Sport and Culture was carried live on national television. When he sat down with Prime Minister Lynden O. Pindling at Government House, photographers captured him autographing "Drama in the Bahamas" T-shirts for the delighted head of state, the same T-shirts vendors were struggling to off-load at his afternoon workouts at the Britannia Beach Hotel.

Yet, if Ali was capable of reprising the performances outside the ring that endeared him to millions, some of the journalists were asking themselves the hardest question of all.

"Why am I here?" wondered Michael Farber in the *Montreal Gazette* on December 10, 1981. "Why is anyone here? We are here because he is Muhammad Ali...and he always will be Muhammad Ali, even if the mountain has come to Muhammad and landed squarely in his stomach. If he loses his 10-round fight to Trevor Berbick tomorrow night, he can always get a job as Santa Claus. We are here because he is Muhammad Ali… and because of the attendant mythology that surrounds him like the 'Yes Champ, no champ' roadies and toadies. We are here because he is Muhammad Ali…and because this is a death watch, a figurative death watch to all but a handful who believe Berbick—the awkward Canadian and Commonwealth heavyweight champion—can do serious damage with his fists."

Farber's take was not out of kilter with the prevailing mood in the wider boxing community. United Press International interviewed five prominent personalities in the game and the opinion of each betrayed the growing anxiety about Ali's fate and health.

"Reflexes and the body are not the same at thirty-nine as they are when you're twenty-seven or twenty-nine," said Alexis Arguello, WBC lightweight champion. "I think somebody is pushing him. He should enjoy the money he has made. He's one of the greatest fighters of all time. He could get hurt."

This was also the take of Ray Arcel, former trainer of Roberto Duran.

"It's a tragedy he's got to fight," said Arcel. "What's he got left? Judging from the Holmes fight he has nothing. I'm really troubled by this. It's a damn shame. There's no reason in the world he should fight. He should enjoy the fruits of his efforts. It can't be money. He could make money in a lot of different ways."

Promoter Dan Duva was of a similar mind.

"It's a disgrace," said Duva. "I think he's being exploited by a lot of people that don't care about him."

Even Don King, not a man known for being overly burdened by matters of right and wrong, had qualms.

"He's made a decision," said King. "If he wants to fight, I'm with him. As far as his right to fight, he shouldn't be denied. But as a fan and as his friend, I'd rather he didn't. Ali has a lot of talent. Like everybody, I'll just have to wait and see. Berbick's strong and a good fighter."

In this particular survey, the only upbeat viewpoint came from Sugar Ray Leonard.

"You can't tell a man, 'don't fight!'" said the reigning welterweight champion. "If he's capable, then let it be. He's been an example to boxing. If he thinks he can do it, then there's no reason he shouldn't. I'll be watching the fight."

Four weeks before the fight, Trevor Berbick had been in Toronto doing his bit to promote the event. With so many people voicing opposition to Ali getting back in the ring, the man due to face him was put on the spot and asked why he signed on for the job.

"Because this is a win-win situation all round," said Berbick. "This fight will get so much publicity all over the world that my name will be known everywhere and can only help my career. I want to give this man, a man who's a legend in his own time, a chance to prove that he can get his body in shape."

An honest answer, it was difficult to fault the logic of the first half of it. Those around him recognized that even a defeat by Ali had unique merits.

"Sure, a loss would set Trevor back," said Irv Ungerman, one of Berbick's advisers. "But look who he'd be losing to—a legend. A man who's known all over the world. He might as well take the chance, if the dollars are there. And he can use it as a stepping stone to perhaps a chance at Gerry Cooney or Mike Weaver."

Those were the very same fighters Ali kept mentioning when discussing his plans for life after Berbick. Whoever would end up taking on the other contenders, there was no doubt that after this bout, regardless of the outcome, Berbick's celebrity would be seriously amplified inside and outside the sport. When you shared a ring with Ali, that came as standard.

For a boxer who'd turned professional in Canada, and had fought only twice outside his adopted country by that point in his career, here was a chance to belatedly announce himself to an international audience. Even if many fans were turned off by the idea of watching Ali go ten rounds with anyone at this stage, they would still read reports about it and absorb coverage and, by osmosis, learn something about his opponent. And, every boxer that ever faced Ali knew they would, at the very least, end up as an entry on the most famous résumé in the history of the sport.

The prospect of becoming a footnote, or perhaps even an end-point in this most illustrious biography, wasn't much consolation to Berbick when he first touched down in Nassau. Quickly, he discovered the basic facilities and equipment that he'd stipulated in his contract were unavailable. The disorganization pointed to James Cornelius and was typical of the way everything was arranged around this bout, but Berbick reckoned he was the victim of gamesmanship by the Ali camp.

"Cornelius is an Ali man," he said, as it became obvious he was going to use the perceived slight as motivation. "There have been some technicalities coming from the Ali people. I was told everything was being set up, but when I got there I had to train at the YMCA and nothing was good enough."

The technicalities included the YMCA not having enough space for him to spar or even to do rudimentary floor exercises. Aggrieved at this, he'd moved to the neighboring island of Freeport where he had friends. There, he set up camp at the Bahamas Princess Hotel, a far more salubrious place than his original lodgings.

If this hardly represented a massive inconvenience, it was enough for Berbick's always readily available paranoia to kick in. Aside from guaranteeing he'd be down to 215 pounds by the weigh-in, he confessed to being gravely concerned about whether the referee would be a strong enough character to stop Ali from pulling him into clinches and stopping him from boxing.

"Ali will try all his tricks, hold and grab and stick his thumbs at me and twist my arms, all the stuff he does. He can only get away with it if the referee lets him. He never learned interior fighting. He always depended on rope-a-dope, on dancing, but he can't dance ten rounds any more. He's too old. He'll try to grab me, and if he does I'll do the same to him. But I hate to do it. I don't think that's the way you ought to fight. In my fight against Holmes, I never grabbed Larry once."

What of the whispers Ali wasn't exactly committed to his training?

"I won't be turned off by negative reports. People tell me Ali is sparring good and that he's in good shape. All I know is that it's an important fight for me. Weaver says he will be glad to fight the winner of this fight. I heard he's waiting for the winner."

Asked what he thought of Joe Frazier's draw with Jumbo Cummings, Berbick answered, "I just read a clipping of it. What he wants to do is his own business. You can't criticize. He should do what he wants to do. I think they gave him a draw, but I didn't watch the fight."

Against the background of Frazier's charitable draw, though, Berbick was definitely worried about the potential for the judges of his contest to award the fight to Ali out of sentiment, or in order to please the crowd.

"When you fight Ali, you fight the entire people around him," said Berbick. "The Muslims, Dundee, and all the people paid to protect him. I can beat this turkey."

Befitting somebody willing to disrespect a three-time champion with that kind of defamatory language, he boasted to reporters he hadn't studied any Ali fights on tape. In what can be interpreted as either ignorance or insolence, or a combination of both, he protested there was nothing more he could learn from going over film of a fighter he'd been watching for just about all of his life.

Contradicting himself somewhat, Berbick later admitted that as a child in Jamaica he'd actually listened to most of Ali's fights in the 1960s on the radio, rather than seeing live pictures. Not that his relative isolation insulated him from what Ali achieved. Indeed, he even attempted to put his opponent's twenty-one year career into a proper historical context.

"Ali took a page right out of Jack Johnson's book. There is always a first in everything in life, and if you think about it Jack Johnson was like that, a real hero."

While so much of Ali's spiel in the extended buildup had included references to the incredible reach of his fame, and his impact far beyond the sporting milieu, Berbick offered a sobering response when asked about how much he and his compatriots looked up to him as a civil rights icon.

"We didn't grow up in an anti-slavery attitude in Jamaica. We had slavery in the past, but we didn't have to talk about it all the time. We could look around us and see black lawyers and doctors and prime ministers. I'm not saying Ali wasn't a hero to me because he was. But when I grew up, I realized that you didn't have to be a loudmouth, either."

If the media were looking to pitch this as a contest between a fighter and the champion he worshipped as a boy, or as a boxer looking to take down an icon whose legend had influenced the path of his own life, Berbick wasn't cooperating much with the narrative.

"I see myself as my own hero," he said.

The clichés he resorted to made him sound like a man trying not to dwell on the persona of the fighter he was facing. Whether this was by accident or design is difficult to know, but he was certainly talking a good game.

"I feel pretty good. It's just like any other fight. I got to be ready mentally and physically. There's no such thing as an easy fight. I never go into a fight looking for an early knockout. I'm just going to box to win. Whatever comes I take it."

Was he concerned that Ali might be able to intimidate him in the ring, psyche him out in the moments before the fight with facial expressions and the famous wide-eyed stare?

"I don't know if that'll help him. I think he's just trying to psyche himself up when he does that. It doesn't matter to me."

At nearly all times, Berbick kept up a very matter-of-fact tone when discussing the task at hand, even offering this very succinct appraisal of what he believed was about to go down:

"'I know he's serious to make a good fight. He wants to make a good payday, and he wants to win. He's had his time, he's made good money, and it's my turn now. I will not feel sorry for him unless I get way ahead and feel that he's being hurt. Then I'd use my discretion and signal to the referee to stop the fight. I've done it to several fighters already. He wouldn't be an exception."

Berbick had much more confidence in his ability to best Ali than he did in the promoters running the show. Basing himself in Freeport had turned out to be a smart move, because being away from Nassau meant he wasn't privy to the various problems besetting the event. As fight night drew nearer, however, he got wind that all was not right. Reporters told him stories of chaos and tumult surrounding the venue, but he didn't need those to know something was wrong. One day before the weigh-in, he still hadn't received a significant portion of the money he was due. He was owed a sizable enough sum for him to threaten to withdraw his services.

"I won't go in the ring Friday unless they give me a letter of credit," Berbick told George Vecsey of the *New York Times*.

He made the short flight to Nassau on the night of Wednesday, December 9, ahead of Thursday's weigh-in. The moment he touched down, he realized sourcing a letter of credit was going to be a lot more difficult than just asking for it. While he had been diligently preparing in Freeport, the international media had started to figure out that James Cornelius was seriously out of his depth, money was a scarce commodity, facilities were substandard, and that the entire promotion was floundering.

"We wanted Muhammad Ali to get back in the ring, and that's what we accomplished," said Cornelius to reporters on Tuesday afternoon.

Any hope that such a statement might mollify the press pack had been misplaced.

"What kind of business are you in?"

"I don't have any businesses," said Cornelius. "I'm a poor man."

"But if you're poor, how are you promoting this fight?"

"I'm through answering questions. Don't ask me any questions!"

And then he stormed off.

Cornelius was taking hits from all sides. Even Ali had started using the phrase, "if the fight comes off," when talking to the media.

Cornelius had also come to blows with Ali's cornerman, Bundini Brown, in an argument about expenses. Betraying his lack of experience,

Cornelius had asked everybody staying in the hotel not to run up massive bills on the promotion's dime. Some in Ali's entourage were legendary for the sums of money they were able to charge to their rooms over the years. When Brown took exception to being called out on his expenditure— he was having such a good time in Nassau he ended up fathering a son (who'd be christened King Solomon Brown) during his stay—the two men had to be pulled apart after some pushing and shoving.

Herbert Muhammad, Ali's manager, was asked what he knew of Cornelius's background.

"He's a promoter," said Muhammad. "He promotes something, I don't know what."

Hardly the most emphatic endorsement and grist to the mill of journalists now starting to believe that Cornelius was incapable of making the bout happen. Suddenly, there were a surfeit of headlines describing him as "the mystery promoter."

Meanwhile, as that flak was flying, Cornelius was, to his credit, actually working to try to ensure the fight would go ahead. In the course of his time in the Bahamas, he'd been introduced to Victor Sayyah, a wealthy American businessman who just happened to be in Nassau that week, somebody he eventually identified as the potential savior of the operation.

"Victor was a handsome man with keen features," wrote Cornelius. "He had a small scar on the right side of his face, which was enough to dispel any thoughts I might have about deceiving him. As we talked, I sensed the gentleness of this man and found him incredibly straight-forward. I convinced Victor that, with $450,000, I could make 'The Drama in the Bahamas' happen. To my complete surprise, he agreed to work with me beginning the next day."

Why would Sayyah get involved? And who was he? Variously listed in profiles as a Denver oil man, an insurance executive, and an international financier, his business interests at that point included the Gateway Hotel in St. Louis, Missouri, which, with a partner, he'd purchased for $3.2 million earlier in 1981. Definitely a man of means and, perhaps most importantly, somebody wired into the strange way the Bahamas worked—at least when it came to getting things done at a time when the islands were notorious for being corrupt, and for functioning as a way station for drug smuggling and money

According to a *Miami Herald* investigation, Prime Minister Pindling received $200,000 from Sayyah and a man called Sorkkis J. Webbe Sr. in 1981. Pindling's associates claimed the money was an investment in the ailing Bahamian World Airways. That's not much of a justification, since it's generally accepted that the airline had been established in 1969—at the law offices of Pindling and his then partner Kendal Nottage—as a vehicle for hiding or laundering money.

A far more likely explanation for their largesse is that Webbe (who had extensive links to organized crime in St. Louis and Las Vegas) and Sayyah had applied for a license to open a casino in Freeport. Gifting cash to a prime minister renowned for living far beyond his means was the best way of ensuring that application might be successful.

When Cornelius brought Sayyah on board, the two worked out of an office in Bahamian World Airways headquarters. Aside from its links to Pindling and Cornelius's closest political contact, Nottage, BWA was infamous for its association in preceding years with Robert Vesco, a rogue financier and fugitive from American justice.

Dirty money allegedly flowed through this company set up by the man who would be Prime Minister (Pindling), and a member of his cabinet (Nottage), who also happened to be his best friend. Against that background, it's hardly surprising that Nottage and his wife, Rubie, would later be indicted in a Boston court for laundering $5 million, the proceeds from drug trafficking, in league with Salvatore Carauna, a major figure in the New England mob.

If these sorts of connections made the whole place reek of nefarious activities and cast shadows over some of the key participants, the fight was saved by Sayyah's involvement. Suddenly, he was a more prominent figure around the hotel than Cornelius, always carrying an attaché case in his hand as rumors percolated that it contained nothing but the ready cash he was using to keep the promotion alive.

What was in it for Sayyah? How about the goodwill and useful gratitude of the Pindling government? After all, when Nottage agreed to host the fight there's no question he did so with the permission and imprimatur of the prime minister. If the event fell through, especially at this late hour with so many foreigners in town to cover Ali, the island would be turned into an international embarrassment, and the administration might come under greater scrutiny. This may explain why one phone call between Cornelius and Pindling ended with the politician telling him rather ominously, "Get this thing done!"

By Wednesday of fight week, several of the undercard fighters and their handlers began to receive at least part of the sums they were owed, and Sayyah claimed everything was all set for Friday night.

"I don't know anybody who isn't satisfied the fight is going on," he said.

Which was kind of true, except for one person. His name was Trevor Berbick. He was still owed money for training expenses, as well as a chunk of his purse. That was going to continue to be a problem as the clock ticked down to Friday night.

CHAPTER NINE
The Financial Make Weight

*After the Spinks fight, I'm quitting, win or lose. Yeah, I know I said
before that I'm quitting. I'm serious. Why? Age. I'm thirty-six. That's
considered old in boxing. My retirement is overdue.*

Muhammad Ali, June 30, 1978

LYING IN HIS HOSPITAL BED at the UCLA Medical Center in Los Angeles after the Larry Holmes fight, Muhammad Ali decided he wanted
to talk to his old friend, Harold Conrad. A number was procured for
Conrad, then in South Africa getting set to promote Mike Weaver and
Gerrie Coetzee in Johannesburg, and a call was made. Turned out Ali
just needed to tell his pal something important.

"Ali did not say where he would like to fight," said Conrad. "But he
was emphatic that he was not finished."

In the late summer of 1981, before the possibility of a fight in the
Bahamas had been nailed down, somebody in Ali's camp tracked Conrad down again.

"We got Ali a license in South Carolina," he said, "but we're not sure
yet where the fight's going to be. Would you help with the promotion?"

Conrad was an obvious man to invite on board, a promoter and a
publicist with a distinguished résumé stretching so far back he turned
down a job offer from Bugsy Siegel in 1940s Vegas. He'd walked the

streets of Manhattan with Damon Runyon, hung out in Havana with Ernest Hemingway, and was the basis for Humphrey Bogart's character in *The Harder They Fall.*

This was the guy who had corralled a young Clay into that iconic photograph with The Beatles in Miami, and then spent Ali's years in exile battling for him to get his license back. The night of his comeback bout against Jerry Quarry in Atlanta, Conrad was so hands-on that he unfolded chairs in the arena.

"Conrad's finest hour may have been his effort on behalf of Muhammad Ali, when the controversial champion was dethroned and driven into fistic exile for his opposition to the Vietnam War," wrote Budd Schulberg. "Conrad was neither an advocate of black power nor exactly a civil rights activist, but he had been instrumental in getting the young Cassius the title shot against Liston and had become one of Clay/Ali's closest honky friends…."

If ever there was an event that needed the pedigree, credibility, and contacts his name would bring, it was this one. After all, he'd been centrally involved in Ali's fights with Jürgen Blin in Zurich and Al "Blue" Lewis in Dublin. He knew that putting on a show in foreign countries posed a different type of challenge, because everything was hardly ever the way it was supposed to be.

Befitting somebody Don King described as "the nonpareil of sell," it's not like Conrad was afraid to associate himself with odd events. After all, he'd been involved in Evel Knievel's Snake River Canyon debacle in 1974. Still, the sixty-first bout of a boxing career he believed should have ended, at the very latest, in 1978 was a bridge too far for him. He declined to get involved, a refusal that drew the ire of the man from Ali's camp.

"How can you do that to Ali after all the years you've been with him?" he asked.

"Any friend of Ali's should do everything possible to keep him from fighting before he gets seriously hurt," said Conrad.

Of course, the fight had gained traction of a sort without him, and as the date of the contest drew nearer Conrad couldn't help wanting to be there. He'd been present for some of the fighter's finest and darkest hours. The thought of missing out on the farewell, however tawdry, began to jar. Surely, it was only right that he bear witness the night the curtain finally came down on a career with which his own had been so intertwined.

Conrad met Ali on the day he arrived in Nassau. Immediately, his old friend started to give him the usual pre-fight spiel about how hard he'd worked, how well he'd trained, and how good he felt. Anybody else might have been suckered in by the bravado and braggadocio. Not Conrad. He'd been around too long. He'd heard it all before. He'd seen Ali in his physical and mental pomp, so he didn't believe a word of what he was being fed in the Caribbean. And Ali knew it, too. Eventually, he stopped pretending, and instead he made his old friend laugh.

"Them sportswriters keep sayin' I'm slurrin' my words, like I got something wrong with my head. That's crazy."

"But you do slur your words sometimes," said Conrad with the frankness that was the privilege of long-term friendship.

"You know better than that," replied Ali. "That's the way we talk. You listening white, I'm talking colored."

Few people knew the scene around a big fight better than Conrad. Since the fifties, the parties he threw, the headline-generating nuggets (some true, more not) that he fed newspaper columnists, and the stunts he arranged to drum up interest had become part of boxing lore. He didn't need that wealth of experience to realize this was neither a big fight nor a properly-organized one. No, he recognized very quickly that this was something else altogether. And not something he liked the look of.

"I saw faces I hadn't seen around Ali fights in years," wrote Conrad. "It was like some lost tribe coming together for a final sacrifice. I saw a couple of hookers who used to make the fight circuit in the 1970s. They looked the same: tired. There were old fight buffs who looked like they had come out from under the ring where Corbett took Sullivan. And then there were the hustlers. Anytime Ali fought, they'd show up acting like they should have a piece."

Conrad knew what this was about. He identified all the old faces, the charlatans, the hangers-on, the crooks, the shakedown merchants, the types he learned the hard way would ask you your hotel room number just so they could charge stuff to it. They were all moving parts in the great circus, the traveling roadshow that cranked into gear whenever Ali hit the road. Somehow, some way, they had scrambled to this idyllic island in the sun for one more freeloading vacation, one final roll of the dice, one very last hurrah.

The entourage was much in evidence in the ballroom of the Britannia Beach Hotel at midday on Thursday morning, when both fighters appeared for the weigh-in and a press conference. At least that was the original plan. The event morphed into something much less concerned with how much each man was carrying into the ring and more with whether they'd be carrying any money out of it. For all Victor Sayyah's presumed financial muscle, cash remained an issue.

Well, to everybody except Ali.

"I got paid three million, maybe four million," he said when asked about his purse. "I don't know. I'm not worried."

Those numbers were hugely exaggerated. His actual fee was just over one million dollars. But he wasn't lying about not being unduly bothered. He was always about the possibility of glory more than greenbacks.

As Ali made his way to the weighing scales, one of his hangers-on had to clear his path through the crowd. "Back it up a bit please, please back it up. Please back it up."

Wearing a white robe and looking decidedly downbeat, Ali seemed almost disinterested as Berbick took to the scales first. The Jamaican announced his own weight as "218!" with a grin before asking an official, "What you got?" His initial read was right. He clocked in at exactly 218.

With James Cornelius standing closest to him, Ali was a much less animated presence, a stoic, nearly oblivious figure as he took his position and waited for the scales to be balanced. Eventually, it was announced, "Muhammad Ali, 236 and a quarter!"

The heaviest he had ever been for a fight. One more warning sign, as if it was needed.

With his robe back on, Ali was in an uncharacteristically somber mood when he met the press. His face betrayed no emotion, his voice was monotone and perceptibly slower than usual. Not so much slurred, just speaking at a different speed than normal. His was the demeanor of a man realizing this might well be the last time he'd find himself at the epicenter of so much hoopla.

"When it's time to be serious I can be serious, and this is a serious moment. It's no time for play. I may never get this chance again. I got the chance to go down as the greatest boxer, not athlete, in history. I can make so many people wrong. So many writers are going to have to eat crow. I have so many people to beat, not just Berbick. So I don't have no extra time to clown for ya.

"If I came here clowning, you would all write, 'Same old Ali, forty years old, still clowning around.' I don't have time to clown no more. No more Ali shuffle. No more rope a dope. No more predicting. I'm too old. Time is too short. This is serious."

Nobody expected Berbick to joke around, and it was just as well. When reporters gathered around him, he'd put his tracksuit back on and put away his earlier smile. He, too, had serious matters to discuss. Money matters.

"I gotta be concerned about it. I'm a performer and I'm supposed to be paid after the fight. But I need some guarantees. Like usual, before I get in the ring. And I just told my man here, Brother James Cornelius, that he has to have a little money for me. It's not much. It won't be no problem, I hope."

As he spoke, Cornelius was on his shoulder, eavesdropping, then chipping in with his own comments.

"Ain't gonna be no problem," said Cornelius.

"Okay Bro," said Berbick, sounding not totally convinced.

"Ain't gonna be no problem at all," repeated Cornelius, sounding like a man trying to convince himself as much as everybody else.

Relations between Cornelius and the media had been deteriorating all week. The more questions they asked, the less satisfactory the answers he gave, the deeper they dug. Each fresh round of interrogations was met by pathetic attempts to fob off the inquiries. Now, twenty-four hours before the fight, he declared himself off-limits to the press. When he retreated upstairs in the hotel, a couple of the more dogged journalists intent on pursuing him for more answers had their paths blocked. The promoter might have been struggling to pay the fighters and the hotel bill, but he had retained a quartet of bodyguards that weren't brooking any arguments. They were his security cordon from then on.

Perhaps spooked by Ali's downbeat persona, somebody asked Berbick whether he would ease off if he sensed his opponent was in trouble in the ring.

"Sure," he answered. "You're not here to try to kill somebody."

Sensing a story bigger than the statistics of the weigh-in, a phalanx of reporters accompanied Berbick on his walk back to his accommodation at the Harbour Cove Hotel, peppering him with more questions about whether he might pull out of the fight.

"They have a little problem. They have to come up with all the money, even if they have to go and break the bank. They've already violated four or five parts of the contract dealing with training facilities, food, and transportation."

Would you accept Cornelius's word as a guarantee that you will be paid, asked one reporter.

"Are you crazy?" replied Berbick. "There's a lot of money around here. They can go rob a bank."

He was right about some money being at hand. Greg Page's attorney Bruce Miller said his client had been paid. Not just that, he boasted that he'd been paid in full.

"Either Cornelius came up with the letter of credit to Chase Manhatttan yesterday, or we walked," said Miller. "We checked with Chase and it's there."

Against that, though, Jay Edson had flown in from Florida to serve as one of the judges of the main event. A referee with forty-five title fights on his résumé, Edson had to pay his own airfare from Tampa to Nassau, the first indication he had that this was not the typical Ali fight. He complained loudly that he hadn't "seen a cent" from the increasingly elusive Cornelius.

That sort of talk wasn't doing much for Berbick's mood. To that point, he had only received $100,000 of the $350,000 he was guaranteed.

"I ain't worried," said Berbick. "It's just that I ain't got my money. I got to be concerned, because I'm supposed to be paid before the fight. But I'm business sharp. I'll stay here till I get it, till my banker says it's in the bank. I'll do everything else, but I won't go in the ring until it's certified okay in the bank. They haven't paid me for training facilities, for food, for transportation arrangements for some of my people."

"Do you think they'll come up with the money?" he was asked.

"I think they will," he said.

"What if they don't?"

"Sad story, man. Sad story."

The nearer the fight came, and the more likely it seemed it might never happen, the more philosophical Berbick grew. Aside from legitimately carping about being stiffed, he reflected on how far he'd come on his own journey in language that was, at times, almost Aliesque.

"When I was a teenager, being from a black country, a Third World country, we got so much influence from North America, it was brainwashing, looking up to those people only 'cause you were seeing them and reading about them all the time. I felt, 'I'm from a small island. I'm born into limitation. My country has a government, it has ministers, a parliament like any other country, but it is small, and that means it isn't good enough.' Even Canada, the Americans think it's a second-class country compared to the average ego-type American citizen.

"I got to where I am, where I belong, and I did it myself. I knew this would come if I played my cards right. I had to manipulate the ratings. Being from Canada, I didn't get no justice. You have to be from the States to get the good number ratings. I got no connection with the big promoters like Bob Arum and Don King. I did it all by myself. My parents didn't want no part of boxing, but I grew up and I was of age; I could see the business and see what I wanted. All I wanted to do was be successful, fulfill my dreams."

A follow-up question about why exactly he fought for a living prompted an interesting response.

"It's different. It's not just like any sport. You want to prove you can do what the other man can do. There's a lot of pride and ego involved. It's just something that men have set out to do. It's a test of your manhood—to fight and be a winner. The smarter fighter is usually the winner, and as a professional there are a lot of dreams and goals and money involved. It's a masculine thing. It's what men do."

At least it's what they sign on to do in return for money. And when the money doesn't appear, that's when the problems start. Late on Thursday night, the situation remained unresolved, and the talk around the place was that Renaldo Snipes, another heavyweight contender, was being lined up as a replacement opponent should Berbick opt out.

"I'll fight Ali for 800," quipped Snipes.

"That shouldn't be too hard to arrange," said Allen Abel of the *Toronto Globe and Mail.* "Even Cornelius should be able to raise $800."

"I meant $800,000," laughed Snipes. "Add a few more zeroes, man."

As a last resort, Cornelius went to Berbick's room that night, and an enterprising reporter from Miami managed to hide in a closet to eavesdrop on the encounter. It was a noisy and ill-tempered affair. Berbick had received a letter of credit, but it was for less than he was owed. Insults flew back and forth, one of them persistently pounded a table in frustration, and it culminated, not in the payment of any money, but the slamming of a door.

As December 11, fight day, dawned, Berbick was still owed big and still talking about not putting on the gloves. When he sat down for lunch that afternoon, with journalists present to monitor the ongoing chaos, he ordered two steak sandwiches and quaffed glass after glass of ice tea, each one filled with generous spoons of honey. Then, he requested a third slab of red meat and some chicken.

"Well, at least this stuff hasn't affected your appetite," said his trainer, Lee Black. Behind the gag, there was concern he was eating like a man not getting ready for a night's boxing against Muhammad Ali.

Eventually, as the afternoon wore on, the difference between the letter of credit and the amount he signed on for was sourced. There are differing accounts of who exactly stumped up the missing sum.

"Trevor needed some guarantee of money," said James LeVitus, chairman of SelecTV, who claims he presented him with a letter of credit drawn on Barclay Bank. "We agreed to pay him directly, rather than pay him through the promoters. We didn't give him a penny more than he would have received."

Another eyewitness described Berbick clapping his hands with glee when he opened his hotel room door and found Victor Sayyah and his briefcase, presumably full of cash, standing outside. Whoever, however, he got paid.

Shortly before 6:00 p.m. on fight night, four hours before Berbick was due in the ring, Lee Black confirmed that his man would be lacing up his gloves and taking on Ali. They could not have cut it any closer.

While Berbick fretted and frowned right up to the last, the day of the fight dawned differently for two other main players: James Cornelius and Muhammad Ali.

Cornelius began December 11 just like every morning, on his knees, facing Mecca, praying. On this particular occasion, his supplications had special purpose.

"I asked the Almighty to overlook my shortcomings and to guide me and direct me to his ways. Had it not been for my faith in God and the support and understanding of my family, I would never have made it this far. I wanted the Father to know that I was truly thankful for all the many blessings he had bestowed upon me, including good mental and physical health and a warm and loving wife and sons. I had betrayed God so many times during the last several months, but I had always asked for forgiveness, and I was prepared to accept the consequences of my acts.

"When I had toiled and endured, when everything seemed hope-less, God was due the credit for having made it possible for me to achieve this enormous task. 'Please God,' I prayed, 'stay by my side and show me the light. I am deeply indebted to you for all that you have done for me, and I now ask that you give me the power and the resolve to see this project through.'"

Cornelius had special reason to give thanks. After all, his name had been all over the international press over the previous few days, every story dubbing him a mysterious and enigmatic and dubious character in this drama. Hardly what somebody would want who'd begun his adventure in Los Angeles almost twelve months earlier working under a fake name to try to stay one step ahead of the federal authorities on his trail. He may have been sanguine about the fight happening, and feeling a certain satisfaction that against so many odds, he had pulled some sort of promotion together; but he must also have known his cover was, now, well and truly blown.

Ali, of course, appeared pleasantly oblivious to the logistical disaster going on in his midst. He was also, perhaps for the best, insulated from the American and international newspapers whose coverage during the buildup wouldn't have done much for his ego.

"Trevor Berbick, rough and strong at age 27, should handle Ali easily Friday night," wrote Dave Anderson in the *New York Times*. "But if Ali somehow survives the 10 rounds with the Canadian heavyweight champion, who grew up in Jamaica, and if the old Ali shows even a few flashes of the young Ali, cynics would not be surprised if he were awarded a sentimental decision.

"But even if Ali were to get a decision, he would have to show much more than he did 14 months ago in 10 dreary rounds with Larry Holmes to avert suspicion of an arrangement that would enable James Cornelius to make some big money from promoting an Ali-Weaver title fight."

Under the harsh but fair *Washington Post* headline, "Prospects slim for Ali who isn't," Dave Kindred envisaged the bout in even starker terms:

"Anyone mining for truth around a Muhammad Ali fight soon bends his pickax on the impenetrable skulls of the perpetrators," wrote Kindred. "This is the truth. Prospectors have worked the Ali ground to death, and besides a headache that won't quit, all we have to show for it is the same old thing. The body is 39 and counting, but Ali's imagination is forever 16 and overheated.... Let's say Ali gets in with Berbick, a big, strong, young roughhousing brawler, then what? Some ringsiders consider blindfolds appropriate attire Friday night; not for Ali, for them. They have seen the emperor naked too many times."

In the *Toronto Globe and Mail*, Allen Abel didn't spare the rod either:

"More likely, it will be a dozer of a fight, 10 rounds of flinching and clinching, and suitable evening wear would be Pajama in Bahama. Berbick is strong but slow, the kind of target Ali once stung at will. The fading champion, his mouth full of marbles, says that his mere presence will scare Berbick to death, but this is more a slandering of the opponent than a tribute to Ali's vanished skills. Tomorrow they meet at second base, an old pug with too much pride and a young one with not nearly enough, and in the warm rain it has come to this."

The most lyrical and hard-hitting piece came from Hugh McIlvanney in London's *Observer*:

"He continues to recite the commentary for an epic but what we are seeing is not so much a B-movie as a cruel cartoon," wrote McIlvanney. "Muhammad Ali can still preach and philosophize, boast and charm and predict. What he can't do is fight, at least within a light year of what he once did. The genie is gone from the bottle forever and Ali is ready to be dumped along with the rest of boxing's empties. To do a little dumping at the Queen Elizabeth Sports Centre in Nassau, Trevor Berbick won't have to prove himself an exceptional heavyweight. He will just have to show that he is fairly good at being young."

As some of the finest sportswriters of their generation were viewing the fight through such a gloomy prism, one broadcast journalist was afforded a unique insight into Ali's mindset.

Pat O'Brien was working the fight for CBS. The network had passed on buying the rights, but knew that Ali remained box office enough that they should have a team on site to cover the match, just in case. O'Brien knew Ali through a mutual friendship with Reverend Jesse Jackson Jr. back in Chicago. And, even though he and his crew were contractually precluded from filming any of the fight itself, he knew that the personal relationship would be enough to gain him an audience. Ali was famously generous like that.

That is why, on the morning of December 11, 1981, O'Brien did what any intrepid reporter would do. He strolled along the beach until he reached the villa to which Ali had moved in the days leading up to the fight. He knocked on the door and was invited in for cereal by Ali himself. It's a scenario almost impossible to imagine today. The world's most famous athlete, hours away from stepping through the ropes to fight, answers his door to a television journalist, rustles up some breakfast, and starts gabbing.

In Ali's world, things were always different. He loved company, thrived on an audience, and feared boredom. No sense with him of a man needing or wanting to be cloistered away to get his game face on. Even by his own legendarily loose standards, though, this was a peculiarly relaxed environment. At one point, O'Brien, conscious of it being the day of the fight and having prep work to do himself, got up to leave.

"No, you stay here," said Ali who then began running through the full panoply of his magic tricks.

"Something about that day was both sad and happy," wrote O'Brien decades later. "Clearly, he was nervous. Clearly, he needed somebody to talk to. Clearly, I was at the right place at the right time. We went for a long walk on the beach and the fight never came up. He wanted this fight, and, in his mind, needed to win this fight, but I could see the Ali bravado was falling short of the mark he always hit so well."

Eventually, it came time for them to part. A slightly bemused O'Brien returned to his hotel, and Ali went off for his pre-combat siesta. He was awakened at seven by one of the staff working in the house. By that time, Gene Kilroy, his business manager/facilitator, and Harold Conrad were downstairs waiting for him. He beckoned them to his bedroom, where he lay under the covers watching a tape of Larry Holmes and Berbick that he'd just put in the VCR.

The volume was almost all the way down, and when an animated Angelo Dundee joined the gathering a few minutes later he provided a commentary on the action.

"See that, champ," he said. "He throws everything from the outside. He's wide open down the middle."

A few beats of silence, then more analysis.

"There it is again! Wide open right down the middle."

"Right," Ali said. "He don't throw no straight punches."

"You go into him right down the middle," said Dundee. "This guy's a hound, hear what I'm saying?"

At last, this close to the contest, Dundee had Ali engaged, watching tape and listening to instructions. At least until John Travolta arrived. The star of *Saturday Night Fever* and *Grease* bounded into the room, hugged Ali, and threw himself onto the bed. If the actor seemed delighted to be in the inner sanctum, Dundee wasn't thrilled by his presence. Not when he was trying to get real work done, to get Ali thinking about the night ahead.

"Look at that," said Dundee, pointing at Berbick as round three unfolded on the screen. "That would have been the spot right there. Wide open."

"Gotcha, boss," said Ali.

He hadn't gotten it. His mind was now elsewhere, chatting to Travolta. Any chance of Dundee salvaging the situation disappeared for good when Ali's four children came running up the stairs. Rasheda and Jamillah, the eleven-year-old twins, leapt onto the bed and started kissing him. Nine-year-old Muhammad Jr. copied their act, while thirteen-year-old Maryum watched the action unfold. Even amid this mayhem, Dundee continued to fight his losing battle.

"You got to throw the big one right off the bat," he said, but only Conrad, enjoying the insight into the trainer's strategy, was really listening now. Everybody else was watching Travolta messing around with some oversized Bugs Bunny teeth in his mouth.

"People see me walking through the lobby wearing these," said the actor, "and they say, 'Is that really him?'"

Still, Dundee kept up the stream of advice, desperate to pass on vital instructions.

"The big one, Ali, like we talked about. That will bring out the hound in him."

"Gotcha, Angie," said Ali. "Like I done with Foreman in Zaire." He spoke that line from beneath a pile of kids showering him with kisses.

The tape was still playing when Pat Patterson, Ali's longtime security chief, arrived with Veronica.

"She was wearing velvet toreador pants and a jacket," recalled Conrad, "a lacy ascot and a toreador hat. She looked stunning."

That she was ready to go was the signal for her husband to get a move on, too.

"Getting about that time," said Patterson. "We better get moving. Lots of traffic out there."

Everybody except Ali and his wife went downstairs, where a swollen entourage of family and friends was by now gathered, waiting for the convoy to depart for the arena. Conrad took in the scene, the four black limousines parked in the driveway, the relatives dressed in their finery, and, suddenly, it reminded him of something very different.

"I was about to say, 'This looks like a funeral cortege,' but I bit my tongue."

CHAPTER TEN
For Whom the Cowbell Tolls

I will retire as the first man ever to win the heavyweight title three times and as the first black champion.
Muhammad Ali, New Orleans, September 15, 1978

As THEY WORKED THROUGH THE litany of wrinkles that needed to be ironed out, Shelly Saltman and Phil Gillen eventually pondered the troublesome locker-room situation. The Queen Elizabeth Arena had just two, and they were small and cramped. As headliners, Muhammad Ali and Trevor Berbick were entitled to one each. So was Thomas Hearns, the next biggest box-office attraction. Fitting three into two wasn't even the worst of their mathematical problems. There was also the matter of where to put the raft of fighters scheduled to appear on the undercard.

As was a recurring theme in this event, they improvised, finding whatever they could in the immediate environment and making do.

On his way to the stadium each day, Gillen drove past some RVs parked by a beach. Hardly ideal, but he figured it was worth a shot. When approached, the owners were happy to do business for cash money and free tickets to the fight. The vans were relocated next to the baseball field, where a cordon was fashioned to rope off the space around them so that Berbick and Hearns could prepare for their contests without interruption on the night, albeit in somebody else's hastily borrowed vacation home. To add to the glamour, Saltman had arranged for a portapotty to be placed between the two vehicles.

Since one of the existing locker-rooms had to be reserved for Ali, this meant everybody else was shoehorned into the other. Although the schedule for the evening listed nine fights, the general chaos, the lack of time, and the demands of the television production meant only five ever made the cut. Still, at various points, there were fifteen boxers, their trainers and assorted hangers-on milling around in a space described by the *New York Times* as "a glorified closet." Athletes working up a sweat in that tight an area meant the room was soon hot and fragrant.

"Now I know what the gladiators felt like in Rome," said Scott LeDoux when he walked in. "Ever see the movie *Spartacus?* The gladiators all waited together in one pit. This is unbelievable."

A native of Minnesota, LeDoux was thirty-two, a grizzled veteran with a record of 28 wins, nine losses and four draws that featured defeats by icons of the era like Ken Norton, George Foreman, and Larry Holmes, and a draw with Leon Spinks. One of those fighters whose bravery consistently outstripped his talent; his wholehearted approach to the sport was best captured by his angry response after the ref stopped his fight with Holmes when it appeared his left eye was so damaged he might lose it.

"What's an eye when you've given your heart?" asked LeDoux.

Even for a former college football player like LeDoux, though, the proximity to his opponent on this particular evening was more awkward than usual. All week long, tension had been building between himself and Greg Page, the twenty-three-year-old who at 17 wins from 17 outings was being talked up as a prospect with genuine title potential. At one point, there was an altercation between the pair in a hotel elevator. There followed another testy exchange in the corridors outside the room where, on the afternoon of the 11th, Doctor Perry Gomez was conducting the pre-fight medicals.

"You jerk, go suck an egg," said Page.

"Just make sure that the doctor passes you, so you can show up and get knocked out," replied LeDoux.

"I'll be there," assured Page. "Just be sure you bring the embalming fluid."

That type of rhetoric meant the feud between the pair was simmering nicely by the time they discovered they'd be dressing and preparing within feet of each other.

"I've never seen a promotion this bad," said Page. "Not as a professional. Not as an amateur. Not as a tourist. The whole thing is a game of acey-deucey, a roll of the dice. Whoever is putting on this show is crazy. I've never been on a card with so much chaos. But I'll fight. I'll fight if I have to go out in the middle of the ocean."

In the midst of all the animosity, representatives of Page and LeDoux then had to come together to battle the promoters. As it became more and more apparent that the event wasn't going to start at 6:00 p.m., and that time was going to be at a premium, it was decided their contest couldn't, after all, be scheduled to go twelve rounds. That was, until the Page-LeDoux camps pointed out that in order to be a legitimate United States Boxing Association heavyweight title fight, as advertised, it needed to be set for a dozen.

To those looking for clues that the organizers didn't grasp even the boxing basics, here was more evidence to add to the growing pile.

The Page-LeDoux soap opera was only one of the many storylines playing out in the backstage soap opera. The main plot centered on when the action would actually start. After 6:00 p.m. came and went without any sign of fighters being called to the ring, most people assumed the chaos and tumult earlier in the day was to blame. In fact, there was a whole panoply of other reasons why the warm-up acts were continuing to wait and sweat in the overcrowded dressing-room.

For starters, nobody had thought to order new gloves for the bouts. All the trainers had used gloves in their possession, battered relics bearing the wear and tear of thousands of rounds of sparring, but the promoters were expected to furnish the actual fighting mitts. Which they hadn't. Under pressure, some handlers agreed to let their charges fight with old gloves, but Angelo Dundee and Emmanuel Steward refused to do so.

At the eleventh hour (the preferred time of all arrangements surrounding this event), a phone call was made to Angelo's brother Chris in Miami. A plane was chartered. New gloves were on the way for the headliners. In the meantime, the undercard fights were set to start with the trainers warned not to cut the laces off at the end of contests so the better gloves might be recycled for the next fighters up.

Another problem kind of solved, everything finally appeared ready to go, until somebody noticed one more glaring omission from the equipment required to stage boxing matches. Nobody could find a bell. Because, uh, nobody had thought to bring one.

"It was almost fight time and Clair [Higgins] and I went down our checklist," wrote Saltman. "There was no bell. What were we going to do? Matt Helreich, who worked our publicity and who I hired to be our ring announcer, looked at a cow that was grazing on a pasture near the stadium and cuttingly remarked, 'Maybe you could take the bell off that cow?'"

Saltman and a technician named Jim Potter left the stadium and went into a farmer's field to try to secure a bell for Muhammad Ali's last fight. In true pantomime fashion, Potter was assigned the role of distracting the animal while Saltman busied himself liberating the bell from around its neck. All they needed now was something to hit it with; a hammer was eventually procured from the toolbag of one of the technicians. In a manner that would enter sporting lore, a career that had captivated the world for two decades was going to end in a contest where the start and finish of each round would by tolled by a bell stolen from a cow!

"Whatever else happens, this fight will win the no-bell prize!" said the *Toronto Globe and Mail*'s Allen Abel.

Others didn't see it in such humorous terms.

"This is the tops," said trainer Eddie Futch, when asked to rank the farrago among worst promotions he'd seen. "You don't just jump into your first effort with a big-time fight like this. They don't realize how many details there are that require money. There are so many things they don't anticipate. But you can't say that this gives boxing a black eye, because there are so many promotions that work out wonderfully."

This was not going to be one of them.

As time ticked by, four of the lesser preliminary bouts were culled from the running order. That the canceled contests were listed by the press as "Pete McIntyre vs. Mike Fisher (light heavyweights), Jeff Stoudemire vs. an unnamed opponent (middleweights), Pat Strahan vs. Tony Servance (light heavyweights) and Tony Coster vs. an unnamed opponent (heavyweight)" was one more graphic illustration of the chaotic vein running through the whole affair.

In the end, the truncated undercard was typical of the genre, the usual amalgam of up-and-comers, comeback kids, and journeymen. Yet, on this evening of all evenings, it was apropos that so many of those featured had relationships of some sort with Ali. In one way or another, he'd intersected with or touched their lives.

Growing up on Helen Street on the east side of Detroit, dreaming of fistic glory, Thomas Hearns's boyhood idol was Ali.

Greg Page attended Ali's alma mater, Louisville's Central High School, and, at fifteen, even sparred with his hero for the first time. Thereafter, he was burdened with the unfortunate tag of being "the next Ali." As if there could ever be another one.

LeDoux fought Ali in an exhibition in December 1977, at the Auditorium Theatre in Chicago, a contest in aid of the Children's Institute of Developmental Disabilities, and he'd been regularly mentioned in the years since as a possible opponent in a real fight. Indeed, Ali had once mocked him to reporters, "The White Dope…I mean hope. Oooh LeDoux, can you picture the redneck and the Black Muslim? You're talking about some money. Where's he from? South Africa?"

Earnie Shavers knew exactly what it felt like to take on Ali. He'd faced him down at Madison Square Garden in a 1977 bout so gripping that, according to Thomas Hauser, "more than half of all the television sets in the United States and more than three-quarters of those actually in use were tuned to the fight." Now, just four years down the line, the two boxers were participating in an event none of the major networks would touch, in an arena metaphorically and literally a world away from the erstwhile capital of the sport in Manhattan.

If so many knocking around that baseball field in Nassau could claim some kinship with Ali, none could boast the personal relationship enjoyed by Eddie Mustafa Muhammad. When he signed on to fight Marvin Johnson for the WBA light-heavyweight title in March 1980, Muhammad could cover only minimum training expenses and might have struggled with underwriting his preparations until he received an offer that would change the trajectory of his career.

"A guy by the name of Muhammad Ali said, 'Come to my camp for free. My camp is your camp,'" said Eddie Mustafa Muhammad, who was born Eddie Gregory in Brownsville, Brooklyn, and later converted to Islam. "I didn't even know the man. He paid for my sparring partners and everything else. Just being around him bolstered my confidence. I worked hard and Ali always pushed me, saying, 'You gotta do this and you gotta do that…' We used to box a tremendous amount of rounds. If it weren't for him being there for me I don't know where I would have gone professionally in boxing. He kept telling me you are going to be the best. Bob Arum and the press would always say, 'Why are you so relaxed and confident?' My experience with Ali was why."

After taking Johnson's crown, Muhammad successfully defended his title twice before Michael Spinks had ended his reign the previous July. He had come to the Bahamas on the undercard to take his first step on the long road back. Mike Hardin, a journeyman from Ohio with just two wins from ten professional outings, was his opponent. For somebody of Muhammad's ability, Hardin, coming off five defeats in a row, was as easy a return to the ring as could be arranged on three weeks' notice.

Fittingly then, it was this fighter who had been so positively impacted by Ali who climbed through the ropes shortly before 8:20 p.m. to get the action started on the last night of his mentor's boxing life. Weighing 185 pounds, Muhammad made short work of his task. A right to the face put Hardin down in the first round, a persistent left jab peppered him when he got back up, and another thundering overhand right forced referee Nelson Chipman to stop the fight in the second.

The speed with which the first bout ended pleased the promoters, whose satellite commitments had them frantically counting every second. Next up on the bill were Page and LeDoux, the grudge match that remained, after some wrangling and name-calling, a USBA heavyweight title fight.

All of the arguing about the twelve rounds stipulated in the contract turned out to be in vain. The fight only lasted into the fourth. By that time, Page had shown how cruel boxing can be when it pits a young buck on his way up against somebody almost ten years his senior very much on the way down. It might have ended sooner, except the Louisville fighter was, after all the trash talking between them, relishing putting a beating on LeDoux. He belittled and taunted him throughout, remaining tantalizingly out of reach one moment, then easing in to score at will the next, all while wearing a mocking grin, ridiculing his opponent's best efforts.

With six seconds remaining in the third round, LeDoux, blood leaking from a cut under his left eye, went down for the third time, his legs buckling under the weight of a heavy Page right.

"Are you all right, baby?" asked ref Zach Clayton of LeDoux as he clambered to his feet, literally saved by the bell. The doctor checked him out during the break, and Clayton also visited the corner to warn him, "Show me some more or I'm going to stop it." LeDoux's cornermen asked him if he wanted to quit on his stool. He refused.

Given that the promoters had lured him to the island on the promise of a $40,000 purse, then stiffed him for $30,000 of it, he'd have been forgiven for not answering the bell. But taking the money and running was never his style. He stood up. He boxed on.

At least he tried to. He started the fourth by meeting Page in the middle and letting fly with a wild left that missed by so much his opponent started posturing and mocking him anew. When LeDoux subsequently moved in to attack, Page put him down again with another right and Clayton called the contest. Even as the ref led him back to his corner, LeDoux remonstrated and asked to continue.

"Listen to me, baby," explained Clayton. "I don't want you to get hurt."

Those in the stadium, wondering about what happens when a fighter stays in the ring too long, had just received a disturbing glimpse of what might yet become Ali later in the evening. But there were still two more bouts to come before they would learn if their worst fears on that score could yet be realized.

Hearns was next up. Three months had passed since he fought Sugar Ray Leonard at Caesars Palace in a contest that captivated the sporting world. Some astute judges regarded it as the greatest welterweight bout of all time. In heroic defeat, Hearns trousered $5.1 million and gained the respect of the boxing community, yet losing pained him so much he spent the weeks immediately afterwards not wanting to leave his own house. Now, here he was stepping out of an RV in a baseball field in the Bahamas, wearing gloves that had just been delivered to the gate.

For Hearns, it had been quite a week, from the high of getting in the ring for a sparring session with Ali to the low of standing in the lobby of a Nassau hotel being told he couldn't return to his room until the promoters paid his bill up front. All the distractions counted for naught though as he finally made his way to the ring. This was no ordinary comeback bout either. This was a step up to middleweight, a new departure, a fresh challenge. There was a lot riding on the next few rounds.

Hearns tipped the scales at 155 pounds, ten more than when he faced Leonard. He was still giving six pounds to Ernie "Grog" Singletary, a rugged customer from Philadelphia who'd taken the assignment with less than two weeks' notice. Drafted as a late replacement for Marcos Geraldo, Singletary had to drop nineteen pounds in eleven days to make the fight. In the nature of these things, the legend of his weight loss would grow, later accounts claiming he shed an even more spectacular twenty-five pounds in a week.

"I had to starve myself for the last four days before I fought Hearns," said Singletary. "I didn't really have time to feel prepared for the actual fight."

And yet, what should have been a straightforward return to the fray for the former WBA welterweight champion turned into something a lot more complicated and dangerous. In the first round, a clash of heads left Hearns with a cut over his left eye—no small gash.

"This was the worst cut I ever saw," said his trainer, Emmanuel Steward. "He was gushing blood. It was a terrible cut. I thought this was going to be two in a row that we lost. I thought we were finished, but I got the cut under control."

Hearns emerged for the second round with swathes of Vaseline smeared over his eye, and set about measuring up to Singletary, a true middleweight with 24 wins from 27 fights. As attempts go at proving his credentials against bigger men, this one took time and patience, and turned into something of an education about the new challenges he would face. Singletary had only been stopped once in his career, and although Hearns had been eating an extra meal a day and quaffing protein shakes to bulk up, he still found it difficult to acclimatize.

"Weight makes a great difference," Hearns pointed out later. "I finally realized that. I must have hit him a hundred times with everything I had, but I still couldn't put him down. I was giving away ten pounds [sic], and I realized that bigger guys might carry more punching power but the big thing is they can absorb heavier punches."

Having established a commanding lead on the judges' scorecards from the second round on, Hearns threw everything at Singletary in the ninth, opening a gash over his left eye but still failing to put him down. The Philadelphian was rocked, yet he just wouldn't succumb. The final round was the same story, and even after recording an impressive and instructive points victory, Hearns was annoyed.

"I thought the fight should have been stopped," he said. "The man couldn't see, and I'm not the type of fighter who will hit a man when he's helpless."

While Steward and Hearns went off looking for a surgeon to sew up his face, there was some confusion about the next contest on the bill. Despite earlier reports around the ring that Earnie Shavers's meeting with Jeff Sims had been canceled, the fighters were suddenly announced and on their way to the arena.

"First they told us Earnie was on second," said Jimmy Adams, a former wrestler and then Shavers's manager. "Then they said fifth. Earnie likes to sleep before a fight, so he found a corner and he fell right asleep. Then somebody comes along and says 'Hey, you guys are on in five minutes.' I woke Earnie up, explained it to him, and we went right into the ring. Earnie is no kid, and he needs at least a couple of rounds of shadow-boxing before a fight, just to get loose. He had no time for that."

The lack of a proper warm-up definitely affected him, because Shavers was at a strange place in his career.

By the fall of 1981, he was dabbling in pro wrestling and also working for country singer George Jones. His official title was "executive protection," but his main job was ensuring Jones wasn't living up to his nickname of "No Show" and being waylaid by alcohol or drugs on the way to gigs. Shavers was at the Grand Ole Opry Hotel in Nashville, Tennessee, when he got a phone call offering him a spot on the Ali-Berbick undercard. The promotion was in dire need of credible support bouts, and with Shavers just two years removed from going eleven rounds with Larry Holmes for the heavyweight title, the thirty-six-year-old was a fading star with just enough wattage and lingering name recognition to lift the bill.

"I was offered $50,000 to fight a no-hope opponent who turned out to be Jeff Sims," wrote Shavers. "I couldn't turn it down."

He couldn't turn it down because, like so many other pro boxers, even after seventy-four bouts over twelve years, he'd blown through a million dollars in earnings and hit financial hard times. His family home in Ohio had been auctioned off by the Trumbull County sheriff earlier in the year to pay off debts nearing half a million dollars. A few weeks later, an arrest warrant was issued for him when he'd used a worthless check to buy gold coins worth $9,000. For an aging fighter with a detached retina, a condition that prevented him from being licensed to box in many American states, this invitation to fight on an Ali card seemed almost too good to be true. Which it kind of was.

"We found a sad scene in Nassau, especially where Ali was concerned," remembered Shavers. "He should have stayed retired. I know others said the same about me, but Ali showed visible signs of decline in and out of the ring. The most alarming was that he noticeably slurred his words. His overall movement was much slower, and, clearly, Ali was in no condition to even spar in the gym, much less have a real fight with a strong bull like Trevor Berbick."

Some might have wondered if Shavers himself was wise to be getting in the ring with Sims. A twenty-seven-year-old from Miami with enough punching power to make it to the fringes of the top ten ranked heavyweights, Sims had no great pedigree but he was younger, fresher, and, as his biography (including an infamous run-in with Ali) indicated, also wild and unpredictable. Indeed, even by boxing's traditionally outrageous standards, his journey to the ring that night had been a minor epic.

Born and raised in the maw of rural poverty in Belle Glade, Florida, Sims was picking tomatoes and cucumbers as a seasonal migrant farmworker in Pennsylvania for ten cents a crate when he was eight years old. By twelve his mother was dead, his father had vanished, and he was left to his own devices. At sixteen, he was shot for the first time. In the head. A year later, he killed a man, or as he once described it, "We had a fight, he wound up dead."

Sims wound up in Belle Glade Correctional Institute, serving seven years for manslaughter. He had always known how to fight, but in prison he learned to box, evincing enough talent for the warden to allow him leave the jail on furloughs to fight outside, an arrangement that led to him being crowned the heavyweight champion of Florida. Upon his release, he made his way to the 5th Street Gym in Miami, home of the Dundee brothers and, of course, Muhammad Ali. One afternoon in March 1980, he met the gym's most famous alumnus for the first time. Ali was preparing for a proposed fight with John Tate. Sims was thrilled with the opportunity to measure himself against greatness.

"Ali came into the gym making all this noise," said Sims. "He was talking his stuff about being four-time champion of the world. Then he went to the dressing room. I tried to do his routine. I wanted to intimidate him. I went over and pounded on the dressing room door and yelled for him to come on out. He told Mike Dundee he was going to kick my ass. During the sparring session, he kept talking to me. He told me was gonna run me right out of the ring. He told me, 'So you think you're bad in Florida, well I'm bad all over the world.'

"I was thrilled just to get the chance to box with him. But then he made me mad. He called me a nigger. I told him I'd deck him for that. We really got it on. He's still got something left. He looks to me like a pain freak. The more I hit him the more he wanted. I hit him with some knockout punches, a right to the head, a left to the head, a double left to the body. I hit him more than I ever hit anybody. I didn't want to just put him down. I wanted to bust his ribs, his head. He called me nigger again, and I called him an Uncle Tom for [President] Carter. Then, as he was backing up, I caught him with a left hook and busted his lip. As soon as I saw it was cut, I quit."

In the official version of the story, Ali had spat out his gum shield shortly before Sims hit him so he could deliver his trash talking in a more pronounced fashion, and that exacerbated the damage done. Whatever happened, this was a serious enough cut that it required ten stitches, and left such a telling scar that Ali grew a covering moustache that, as he so exquisitely put it, made him look like "Dark Gable." Some in and around boxing felt the whole debacle was yet one more cogent reminder that Ali no longer belonged in the ring.

Closing in on two years later, Sims was now the final warm-up act as Ali played the part of headliner one more time.

In a suitably bizarre cameo, just as he and Shavers were in the ring limbering up, an attempt was made to get them to climb back out. One of the television producers had decided there wasn't enough time, and tried to prevent the bout from starting so that Ali and Berbick could go on right then.

"I told them, 'No way,'" said Adams. "I told them to get lost. We were going to fight right then and there."

And that's what they did. After ninety seconds of shadow-boxing and playful jabbing, Sims lived up to his reputation as a dangerous puncher, catching Shavers with one of those concussive rights to the jaw that made him fall almost in slow motion. He barely beat the count, then retreated to the ropes, hung on, and played mind games with his opponent.

"Slow down, Jeff, we got ten rounds to go," whispered Shavers to Sims in a clinch, "Put it in low gear, brother."

Whether that was the reason or not, Sims failed to capitalize on the weakened condition of Shavers, who was struggling so much that Adams broke a capsule of smelling salts under his nose to try to rouse him for the start of the second. Still, Sims dominated that round, staggering Shavers with repeated shots to the head and looking capable of adding to his record of 12 knockouts in 14 fights. But, in the end, experience won out. Shavers improved, had Sims down in the fourth, and knocked him out in the fifth.

"Mr. Shavers, you lied to me about going ten rounds," said Sims afterwards.

"Jeff," replied Shavers, sitting in the tiny locker-room the two men and thirteen other fighters had shared that night, "welcome to the big time!"

Elsewhere in the stadium, a group of journalists were crowding outside Ali's locker-room, hoping for some last-minute pre-fight quotes. Howard Bingham came to the door, surveyed the faces, and beckoned Pat O'Brien inside. Quite a coup for the man from CBS, given they had no financial stake in the event, and a decision that didn't go down well with some of his media brethren.

"All hell broke loose," remembered O'Brien. "Dick Young [iconic columnist with the *New York Daily News*] began screaming, 'You motherfxxking, cxxksucking asshxle, get the fuck out of here,' or something close to that, and then someone, maybe him, picked up a chair and threw it at the door. It was crazy. I closed the door, walked over to Ali, and said, 'Got any more magic tricks tonight?' He laughed and said, 'No!'"

CHAPTER ELEVEN

Separating the Dancer from the Dance

I'm thirty-seven years old. For sports, that's kind of old. I want noth-
ing to do with boxing anymore. I'm going on to a new life. Boxing
was my launching pad. I'm in orbit now. The worst thing I can do is
go back in the ring.
　　　　　Muhammad Ali, Albany, New York, January 30, 1979

ANGELO DUNDEE WORKED ALI'S CORNER in a competitive fight for the
first time on December 27, 1960, at the Miami Beach Auditorium on
17th Street and Washington Avenue, a special holiday promotion put
together by his brother, Chris. The then Cassius Clay fought Herb Siler
on the undercard of an event headlined by Willie Pastrano taking on
Jessie Bowdry. In the fourth of eight scheduled rounds, in what proved
a tricky enough encounter, a right to the body and a left hook to the
jaw ended Siler's evening. That prompted his eighteen-year-old opponent, now the proud owner of a 2 and 0 record, to brashly inform the
bemused crowd, "I'm gonna be heavyweight champion of the world."

　　Almost exactly twenty-one years later, Dundee was standing in a
ring with a full moon above him in the Caribbean sky, waiting one more
time for the fighter with whom he'd embarked on an odyssey through

the pages of history. How much time had passed since their first night's work together? Well, the Siler fight was so long ago that in Miami Beach back then, people of color were not allowed in between sunset and sunrise unless they had a pass. Indeed, since facing Ali, Siler had gone to prison for manslaughter, served seven years, and been released back into society as a born-again Christian. Yet, here was Dundee in another arena, in a foreign country, at a different time, still waiting for his man, the boastful teenager from way back then now perilously close to middle age.

With a white towel folded neatly over his left shoulder, Dundee wore his trademark glasses, black pants, and a short-sleeved white smock that made him look half-barber, half EMT. Every pocket of that garment held the tools of his trade: gauze pads, sterile gauze, Q-tips, Aquaphor, and a selection of coagulants that included Adrenalin chloride 1-1000, Avitene, and thrombin. And, of course, his very own concoction: a special ointment fashioned from alum, cornstarch, thymol iodide, and Vaseline. Everything he needed for a night at the office.

Dundee may have been prepared, but he also looked concerned—beyond even the concern every trainer has before a bout. Sure, he had seen it all through the years with Ali and so many other fighters before him, but he knew how badly prepared and unfit to fight his boxer was for this one. Yet, what could he do? Desert him and let somebody less qualified work the corner, or show up and try to save the man from himself? Again.

When Ali began his long walk from the locker room, Bobby Womack was in the ring giving an especially lusty rendition of "America the Beautiful." In keeping with the tone of the evening, Ali's circuitous trip across the running track and the sandy infield was drawn out and chaotic. At first, he was throwing shapes, jabbing, bobbing and weaving as he went, albeit in an almost slow motion style. However, halfway through, he stopped sparring. He may have been worried about fatigue, or he could just have grown disinterested given how long it was taking for him to reach his destination.

Even as Ali was en route, there was yet more logistical drama playing out. At ringside, a troupe of Junkanoo dancers had arrived and were, as previously scheduled, about to climb through the ropes to give a performance. Clad in elaborate, shiny gold costumes, wearing masks and carrying drums and whistles, they were ready to wow the worldwide audience with their native Bahamian culture—until one of the television producers blocked their path, shouted about the cost of satellite time and the event running late, and promptly canceled their routine. Policemen had to be deployed to remove the irate dance company.

This was no ordinary fight night.

"I am seated at ringside, in the assigned chair of the prime minister of the Bahamas," wrote Bernie Lincicome. "I have stripped the adhesive tape with his name—Pindling—on it and put it on the chair behind me. When Pindling shows up with his friends and bodyguards in aviator sunglasses, he sits where I have placed him. The others fill in and muscle innocents out of the way. I have deposed a head of government, at least by one row."

In the ring, Kendal Nottage, conveniently ignoring the disarray going on behind the scenes and sometimes in front of them, was in the ring, describing what was about to happen as "a progressive step for all mankind in the world."

Meanwhile, Wally Muhammad was at the head of the phalanx still trying to push Ali along, strolling through the darkness, the only light in that part of the venue coming from the television cameras tracking the star turn. As the crowd surged constantly towards them to get a closer glimpse, they had to be repeatedly told to "Get out of the way! Get out of the way!" Ali, wearing a white robe fringed with the black, aquamarine, and yellow of the Bahamian flag, finally neared the ring, as a chant of "Ali! Ali! Ali!" went up. It started impressively enough, but faded and trailed off quickly.

When he climbed through the ropes, Ali lifted his hands in recognition of the crowd in the most desultory way possible. The body English was almost apologetic. On the television commentary, Don Dunphy noticed the mood.

"A very serious group around Muhammad Ali," said Dunphy. "Nobody is smiling. Angelo Dundee is the most lighthearted of the group. I've never seen the people around him look that somber. He must question his ability. He must. He's a very rational person."

As if he had overheard, Ali caught Dunphy's eye just at that moment, smiled at him and winked. Then he resumed some slow-motion shadowboxing. He had to do something to keep busy because there was no sign of Trevor Berbick. On a colder than usual night for the Bahamas, Ali was standing around for four full minutes before his opponent finally appeared, Berbick and his entourage almost sprinting from the locker room to the ring.

Referee Zach Clayton called the two combatants and their handlers into the center for final instructions. A mustachioed figure, Clayton was a former Harlem Globetrotter who had officiated "The Rumble in the Jungle" between Ali and Foreman, offering another reminder that the heyday of one of these fighters was long gone.

"Men, this is your fight," said Clayton, still clad in a windbreaker to ward off the unseasonable chill. "All I want is a good clean fight, This morning, your representatives were briefed about the rules and regulations of the Commonwealth. A few of the rules I think it's most important to rehash."

As he reiterated that three knockdowns in a single round would end the fight, Ali looked distracted, winking at someone off camera then shadowboxing in front of Berbick. As Berbick listened and tried not to be intimidated, his trainer Lee Black kept pinching the skin on the back of his neck throughout. Almost as if he needed to agitate him.

After Clayton finished his speech, Dundee shouted, "Take some of that grease off your fighter" in Black's direction. The first note of rancor in the evening, it was almost out of step with the mood which hitherto had been excessively polite and mannered and devoid of the usual bitterness and name-calling that are the hallmark of so many fights. None of that mattered unduly now, because shortly after 11:00 p.m., the cowbell rang for round one.

Ali led off with a couple of stiff left jabs, the weapon he would rely on for most of his offense throughout the night. He started out better, Berbick seeming cagey or nervous or both. Ali delivered a strong left, then a good right in what was a promising beginning that he couldn't keep up. The arms were going okay, but his legs were moving slower. There was no dancing, just labored walking as he shuffled away, especially when Berbick finally began to go on the attack.

"Show me your speed! Show me your speed!" Berbick taunted, as Ali backed away from his assault.

And for the first of many times, Clayton admonished him to stop talking.

As the round wore on, Berbick grew stronger and bolder and started mimicking the way Ali was moving. With just over a minute left, he connected with a tremendous left to the body, but Ali seemed unaffected. The crowd grew excited when Berbick slipped and skidded back into the ropes at one point, but to dampen their enthusiasm he practically sprinted back into the center to restart hostilities.

"Fast hands," shouted Bundini Brown from the corner. It sounded like a plea, more a wish than an instruction.

With another strong left and a barrage to Ali's body, only Berbick's wildness prevented him from doing more damage as he swung punches in great, ungainly arcs. When the cowbell rang, he raised his arms in mock triumph. Maybe taunting a crowd who had made it known they favored Ali, or perhaps enjoying a moment as he realized he was in with a shadow of the "The Greatest," and this was a fight he could very easily win.

On the television feed, Dunphy and Davey Pearl talked up the round, justifiably pointing out that Ali evinced more life in the opening stanza than at any point during his defeat by Larry Holmes fourteen months earlier. However, even three minutes in, Ali was slumped on his stool, so tired and dazed looking that Angelo Dundee had to move his arms off the ropes and down to his side for him.

In the second, Ali started flicking away with his left jab, but from so far back he was unable to reach his target. He was cautiously maintaining his distance, because Berbick, much the livelier combatant, was swinging like a man looking to end the contest early. He repeatedly stalked Ali, who took the punches and then drew him into clutches. The problem was that even during those wrestling bouts, Berbick was continually battering him in the ribs with lefts and rights.

The first clinches had made Ali realize the difference between him and the man he was facing. "When my body went against his, mine was so soft and his so hard."

A minute into the second, the crowd started up another "Ali! Ali! Ali!" chant. Like everything else about the bout during the week, it was halfhearted, a pale imitation of what that chant used to sound like and used to represent.

Hilariously, Berbick responded to the chorus by holding his hands up as if asking the crowd, "Why?" Why indeed? Why favor this American over me, a kid from a nearby island trying to make a name for himself? Of course, they were chanting for history, for the legend, for the era that was going to end before their very eyes.

Appearing angered by the lack of support, the Jamaican went on the attack. Again, he discovered that Ali's ability to hold and frustrate prevented him from doing real damage. Ali's own attempts at offense were so disorganized and awkward that even Dunphy, who had been doing his best to hype up the fare, admitted, "Ali's reflexes are gone."

Long gone. Not even halfway through the second round.

Even his one-two combinations were off, the muscle memory betraying him when he needed it most, the brain writing checks the body couldn't cash. With thirty-four seconds left in the second, he threw his first significant power punch, and the sheer effort of doing so seemed to take its toll on him. After recovering from that expenditure, Ali connected with a couple of hits from long-range and a series of better jabs just before the bell.

The problem was, they scarcely seemed to impact on his opponent, and, at the bell, Ali trudged back to his corner like a tired man. Across the ring, though, Berbick also appeared to be gassed. He spent the interval gasping for air. Just two rounds in and the headline acts were already betraying serious signs of fatigue. A consequence of the troubled buildup? Maybe. It certainly wasn't down to the excessively sapping nature of the combat in those opening six minutes.

At the start of the third, Ali lay against the ropes awaiting the bell, Bundini Brown exhorting, "Go get him, champ!" into his ear. Having started with a wild left that threw him off balance, he recovered to use the jab effectively again and to unleash another decent right. Berbick was definitely shaken by this assault but responded well and smartly, pushing Ali onto the ropes and landing a series of body shots of his own. He had more success in that regard when Ali tried to hold on to him in the middle of the ring, swinging punishing lefts and rights to the ribs.

Each time Ali went on the attack it was all too brief. Berbick was regularly open, but Ali seemed to step back after the second or third punch of every assault, either tired, afraid he'd wear himself out by the effort, or wary of being caught with a big hit. The latter concern was hammered home early in the third when Berbick connected with an excellent left hook that had Ali leaning against the ropes and troubled.

Tellingly, Berbick seemed either unable or unwilling to press home his advantage in these situations, pulling back and away rather than going in for the kill. In between these all too brief flurries, both men stood off each other in the center of the ring for long spells, feigning, bobbing and weaving so slowly, and pawing each other so gently as to make it look almost ritualistic or rehearsed.

For thirty seconds at the end of third, Ali didn't throw a single punch, just tried to fend off attacks, until finally releasing a left as an afterthought at the sound of the bell. As he turned to go back to his corner, Don Dunphy called it as he saw it, "My Goodness, Ali just walked back, reeling."

On his stool, he looked up plaintively like a child, and asked his corner, "Who's winning?"

"You are," chorused Bundini and Dundee. He wasn't.

As Ali made his way out for the start of the fourth, Bundini was shouting again, "Don't hesitate, and when he come in close, tie him up!"

The most celebrated cheerleader in sport, the man responsible for "Float like a butterfly, Sting like a bee" appeared worried, as did everybody in that corner and all over the stadium. And with very good reason. Early in the fourth, Berbick maneuvered Ali into a corner and unleashed a barrage of body punches, genuinely heavy blows. Ali did well just to hang on, as he took several hits to the head, too. Eventually, he escaped, only after taking fourteen punches without offering any in retaliation.

Even then, Berbick remained in hot pursuit and Ali looked to be not long for the fight. The crowd tried to lift him with another short-lived bout of chanting, but he was retreating like an old man suddenly discovering he had no business in this ring on this night, being chased and harried and hurt by a younger fighter.

The fight might have ended right there, except that Berbick was gassed, too. He couldn't sustain the assault and was unable to produce the type of flurry that might have forced Clayton's hand. Ali woke up in the last minute of the round, perhaps sensing that Berbick had grown arm weary. Briefly, the thirty-nine-year-old was up on his toes, landing some punches of his own. None, however, were delivered with enough menace to hurt Berbick who, just before the bell, produced a strong left that sent Ali bouncing off the ropes.

The fifth started belatedly, Clayton admonishing both corners to get out of the ring, each perhaps trying to inveigle crucial seconds of rest for their waning charges. Ali walked slowly, deliberately to the center of the ring, and Berbick sprinted to meet him there. Within seconds, he connected with another percussive left that stunned Ali. Then he spent the next minute bullying him around the ring, flurries to the body and the head punctuated only by Ali stopping the bleeding by holding on with all the survival instincts of a professional of twenty-one years' standing, his left arm snaking around Berbick's neck, drawing him in close enough to limit the damage.

By now, the two fighters were a study in contrast, one moving, alert, animated, pouncing with punches, the other fending off attacks with arms flailing in slow motion, his feet appearing stuck to the canvas.

Berbick did all the running. Ali backed away and away and still was occasionally rocked on his heels. More and more the younger man was able to do as he pleased. A couple of big hits to the body in mid-round might have downed another fighter. Ali stood there, taking it, offering only the most fleeting resistance, his jab by now almost redundant. At one point, it seemed a case of *when*, not *if*, he would fall and/or Clayton would step in to end his suffering.

"Punch out and get out, punch out and get out," said Clayton, stepping in for the umpteenth time to break up a clinch, Ali holding Berbick tightly, desperately, trying to prevent him from unleashing yet more flurries.

With fifty seconds to go in the fifth, after Clayton had dispersed them yet again, Ali finally roused from his latest slumber, resuscitating his left jab and throwing a few combinations. That they scarcely impacted on Berbick didn't matter that much. The mere gesture of intent was enough to fire up some in the crowd. "Ali! Ali! Ali!" There weren't enough voices to legitimately call it a chorus. It was just a couple of men at ringside, offering up a plaintive reworking of a familiar refrain. Like the fighter they were egging on, just a weak version of a famous old classic.

Berbick reacted to this brief barrage with some more wild punches of his own, leaving himself wide open for an Ali left hook that connected with his head. A solid enough punch, but there was no follow-up to exacerbate the damage. With ten seconds on the clock, Ali scored big again as Berbick let his hands drop. This time, the fans were genuinely excited, rising to their feet, urging more from their hero. But the bell tolled. The brief Ali renaissance and his best round of the fight had ended.

"Big round!" shouted Bundini as Ali sat on the stool. "Big round! You got it, I'm telling you!"

"That's number five," said Dundee. "We're halfway home. Halfway home."

Whether it was the cheerleading or his brief heroics at the end of the fifth, Ali definitely appeared in better fettle as he rose for the sixth, showing more purpose, pausing with his hands on the ropes, his eyes staring across the ring.

"Find the target, champ!" urged Brown. "Find the target!"

Soon enough, the target found him.

Ali started the sixth in better fashion than the previous five, more pep to his step, even the jab now being delivered with more snap and intent than before. Again, an "Ali! Ali! Ali!" chant flourished briefly.

"Hearing it was a good feeling," said Ali later. "You're just sorry you can't respond to the cheers like you used to."

Berbick possessed the greater energy and, though he often swung wildly, he also dictated where the combat would take place, pushing and punching Ali back onto the ropes, quickly silencing the fans.

After Clayton had separated them yet again, Ali beckoned Berbick forward with his right fist, exhorting him to bring what he had. Berbick did just that. Seconds later, Ali brazenly taunted him again. The type of flamboyant cockiness that in his prime was such a crucial part of his shtick now just seemed kind of pathetic when his opponent so obviously had the upper hand.

For much of the sixth, though, both men seemed tired. Occasionally, they sized each other up in the center of the ring, offered some poor excuses for punches, then stood off again. Ali's only real offense by now was the intermittent left jab. Berbick had more weapons at his disposal, but none capable of inflicting enough damage to prematurely end the affair.

"Be what you used to be!" roared Bundini, his knack for poetic lines still intact, his shouting now serving as a constant, poignant sound track to the struggles of his friend.

"Ali still takes a punch as good as anybody in the ring," said Dunphy, grasping for something positive to say to those watching on television.

At the end of the sixth, they were tangled up and kept squabbling with no great purpose for a few seconds after the bell, the empty gestures of tired warriors.

At ringside, John Travolta, sitting next to Veronica Ali, was signing autographs for fans at this point in the proceedings. Yards away from where Veronica smiled beatifically for the well-wishers, her husband's back curved as he slumped in the chair, listening to his cornermen urging him to "Go get him."

He opened the seventh on the offensive, throwing a few jabs that grazed Berbick. Fending off that feeble assault, Berbick unleashed a couple of sturdy lefts, one to the chin, another to the body, and Ali, as usual, resorted to holding to tamp the onslaught. Twenty seconds later, however, he had his hands up as Berbick battered him against the ropes. Again, the end seemed near, except that Berbick didn't have the stamina to keep up the attack, and Ali eventually escaped.

Moments later, that scenario repeated itself. Ali leaned against the ropes as if for support to keep him upright, Berbick landing intermittent shots but unable to produce a sustained attack to force the referee's hand. Worryingly, though, other than the odd retaliatory and increasingly perfunctory left jab, Ali was offering little in the way of a counter. With just over a minute to go in the seventh, Berbick went on the offensive again, landing punches at will, each one appearing to stun and hurt Ali. If none were quite weighty enough to put him down, at one juncture Ali looked as if he was going to fall out of the ring as he leaned back over the ropes to try to avoid the punches being rained on him. With forty-three seconds left, Berbick stopped his attack. He looked over at Zach Clayton and shouted, "He's hurt." His eyes as much as his words betrayed how much he was hoping the referee might step in and call a halt to what was by now a one-sided pummeling. This is what Ali had been reduced to, his opponent pleading for the ref to show mercy.

Were it anybody else on the receiving end, Clayton might have. But it was going to take a courageous ref to stop Ali's last fight in these circumstances. So he stayed in there, upright and willing, and his damaged body continued to take a beating. All that he could do to lessen the damage was resort to clinches and holding, temporary abatements. The round finished with Berbick on the attack, Ali struggling to offer any riposte, and so many of those necklacing the ring wishing they were someplace else.

"In the Holmes fight, I kept expecting that moment when he would be the Ali we had seen a dozen times, the Ali who would unleash a flurry of punches that roused the crowd and himself," said Dave Kindred, "It never happened. The difference was, against Berbick, I never expected Ali was capable of anything, let alone a moment when he could turn back time. I believe he knew in his mind he was done. But his great heart wasn't ready to quit."

Jay Edson, the judge from Tampa who'd paid his own airfare, was struggling with the grim spectacle. After every round, he turned to Bernie Lincicome, a journalist he didn't even know but happened to be sitting beside, and said, "I can't do it. I can't give Ali the round. I just can't." Edson was trying to professionally evaluate a boxing match with tears streaming down his face at the plight of one of the participants.

Ali looked dazed as the bell tolled for the eighth, strolling from his corner with his arms by his side. Then, amazingly, he got up on the balls of his feet and started dancing. Like the Ali of old, not this old Ali. The brief interlude wowed the crowd but was brought to a shuddering halt by a heavy left from Berbick. He recovered and restarted the shuffling, resembling a man turning the key in the ignition in the hope that the engine might splutter into life.

"Dance!" roared Bundini from the corner. "Dance!"

The footwork enlivened the crowd enough to spawn yet one more "Ali! Ali! Ali!"

It was an amazing sight. The moribund character from before suddenly, however briefly, resuscitated, even the left jab appearing snappier and more forceful. For all the theatrics of the moment, though, Berbick remained focused on the task at hand. Ignoring the distraction of the sights and sounds of a purported Ali revival, he continued to stalk his prey, moving slowly but with purpose, finding him eventually. He burrowed Ali into corners and against the ropes, and kept up a steady diet of punishment. A right to the head staggered Ali, yet, somehow the legs, perhaps fueled by the noise, had enough in them to help him reverse away from danger.

For all his dancing cameos and the heightened din from the bleachers, Ali lured Berbick in close and then held him in clinches until Clayton made him stop. Midway through the round, Ali was rocked onto the ropes again by a strong left. If Berbick had heavier artillery in his arsenal, it was the kind of direct hit that might even have put Ali down. As it was, he followed that up with another dozen punches, at least half of which reached the target, as a desperate Ali reached out and tried to hug his way out of trouble.

Inside the final minute, Ali unfurled one audacious right hand uppercut, but Berbick saw it coming and smacked it down. As the clock wound down, Ali used his left jab to good effect, and a right cross reached Berbick's head but didn't carry enough purchase to impact. When the bell sounded, the crowd's reaction was that of an audience that had just been allowed a glimpse of what Ali used to be. They had been duped, however. It was his dancing feet and not his punches that turned the clock back and reminded them of younger, more glamorous nights than this one.

At the start of the ninth, Ali rose wearily once more. Bundini Brown leaned over the ropes, slapped him on the shoulders and said, "You can do it, champ, come on now, you can do it!"

But there was no more dancing to fire up the crowd. Instead, the fight reverted to the old narrative, Berbick doing all the work, Ali trying to fend him off with his left jab. When Berbick hit him twice in quick succession, Ali offered up a defiant shuffle just to tell his opponent how little the blows hurt. Nobody was fooled.

"That ain't dancin', that's runnin'!" shouted a spectator at ringside.

Harsh but fair, as Ali did his utmost to keep away from Berbick, who enjoyed most success when he backed his man onto the ropes. With forty seconds left until the bell, that's exactly where Ali was when Berbick picked him off at will. Another sustained round of suffering. The only respite came when he could wrangle him into a clinch or deter him with a jab that was tiring and increasingly falling short. The round ended with Ali taking too much punishment, trying in vain to get his hands around Berbick's head as Clayton reprimanded him, "Punch out or get out!"

When the bell finally rang, Ali lingered in the center of the ring. He stared at Berbick, who walked back to his own corner with his hands raised above his head, perhaps confident now that victory, no matter what the judges' hearts might want them to do, was firmly in his grasp. The look Ali gave was more of fond bemusement than anything approaching malice. Then, belatedly, he turned and straggled back to his corner to prepare for the last round of his life.

As Dundee squeezed a water sponge so the cool drops spilled down on Ali's head, Don Dunphy captured the feelings of all sane people watching this spectacle, "Win, lose, or draw, I hope he doesn't fight again." To which his co-commentator Davey Pearl added, "I pray he doesn't."

"Three minutes," shouted Dundee. "That's all!"

"We got this!" urged Bundini.

Then the cowbell tolled, an unfamiliar clang but one that signaled the start of the last round of the most fascinating fistic career. Clayton beckoned both men to the center, where they touched gloves. "Go! Go! Go!" shouted Dundee, and Ali danced away. But wherever he went Berbick soon followed, chasing him down and letting fly, swinging a little too wildly, but the sheer quantity of punches meant some still hit home with purpose.

Thirty seconds into the round, Ali, perhaps figuring a knockout was his only hope, planted his feet and tried to go toe to toe. He landed a quick combination, the sheer effort of which seemed to fatigue him, so the tactic was short-lived. When he found himself back on the ropes soon after, his attempt at another combination was so labored that it appeared to be delivered in slow motion.

Halfway through the round, the crowd found its voice again and started up perhaps the most sustained and noisiest "Ali! Ali! Ali!" of the evening. Maybe the sound of that lifted him because, from somewhere down deep, he found reserves of strength to attempt some more flurries.

The more animated he became the livelier Berbick's response, bullying him around the ring with the speed of his attacks. At one point, he was beating Ali up in his own corner, the former champion almost bending over double to avoid the punches. When he did counter, his efforts were painfully slow and ineffective. He attempted a haymaker with his right, the effort of which nearly caused him to fall over.

Through it all, Berbick just kept coming and coming. Only the fact he didn't possess the skill to land more accurately was perhaps the main reason why Ali remained upright

Ali spent the last ten seconds, of the round, of the fight, of his boxing life, on the ropes, taking hits and offering little in the way of riposte. At the bell, Clayton coerced both men into an awkward hug over by Ali's corner. As Dundee went to cut off his gloves, Ali's face was a mixture of sadness and perhaps shock. There was no hint of the mischief or the effervescent smile. Was it regret at coming back, sadness at suffering yet another loss, or the realization that he'd never fight again?

He wasn't alone with his thoughts for very long as the ring was soon swarmed with bodies. Amid the ensuing chaos, off to the side, Bundini produced a comb from his pocket and handed it to Ali, who very calmly ran it through his hair. Regardless of the result, he was going to be ready for his close-up.

As they waited for the decision, Bundini and others in Ali's extended entourage were hugging each other as though they were celebrating an imminent victory, and telling onlookers their man had definitely won. Were they doing it for the cameras? Were they that myopic? Was the delusion maybe for Ali's benefit? Whatever the motivation, they can't have believed what they were saying.

"The ring must be cleared or we cannot have a decision," said Matt Helreich on the PA. "We must clear the ring, please. All newspaper and photograph people, please clear the ring. You'll all be given a chance later. We cannot have a decision until the ring is cleared."

With no sign of the crowd dispersing, or of a decision being announced, Davey Pearl made his way to the ring where Berbick was standing in his corner, telling members of the crowd, "I didn't try to hurt him, I just want to win. I hit him with all right hands, and all I could think of was the man getting hurt."

Davey Pearl walked over and put a microphone in Berbick's face.

"How you doing?" said Berbick, flashing a smile. "I'm waiting on this decision, I know I won the fight, there's no doubt about it. This fight was awful. Since I got here, it was a mental strain they put me through. It hurt me mentally so bad that physically I'm tired. I survived and I overcame, I know it."

"Earlier in the fight, you were talking to him," said Pearl. "What were you saying?"

"I just told him do the best you can, I don't want to hurt you."

An answer that cut to the heart of the whole charade.

After a fashion, some but not all the interlopers eventually vacated the ring so the verdict could, finally, be delivered.

"Ladies and gentleman we have a unanimous decision," said Helreich. "Judge Alonzo Butler votes it 97-94, Judge Clyde Grey votes 99-94, Judge Jay Edson, 99-94, a unanimous decision for Trevor Berbick."

"I did it!" shouted Berbick with almost childlike glee, beaming as his corner hoisted him in the air. "That's all I wanted to do was win."

Across the ring, Ali wiped his face—for once expressionless—with a white towel, then slowly began to walk to meet his conqueror. Berbick enveloped him in a hug and roared in his ear.

"I shall go on to win the world championship. Wait till you see me next time, I will shine. You were my superior, but I'm going to do it for you, man. You've inspired me since I was a kid. I love you, man! You are a true brother, thank you, man…. You made me, bless you…. I will pray for you."

Ali didn't speak. He just smiled ruefully, and then he turned to leave. At this point Jim Hill corralled him with a microphone.

"Can I get you for a second, please?" he asked, his tone apologetic, as if conscious of intruding upon the grief.

"Some people at ringside thought you might have won this thing?" asked Hill, bizarrely.

"It was close," said Ali, his voice barely discernible with the din of the crowd still milling around. "It was close, but I have to submit to the judges. He was strong. He was good. I think he won."

As he finished his answer, he turned to where Berbick was mouthing streams of consciousness in the other side of the ring, and smiled. He was that soldier. Nobody ranted and raved in victory better.

"Do you agree now, Muhammad, that you should retire and never come back in this ring?" asked Hill.

"I'm sure that this is enough to convince me. I didn't get hurt. I saw the shots but couldn't take them. Father Time just caught me. In my young days, I wouldn't have had much trouble, but I think time caught me. This is it. I'm sure I'll wake up next week saying I'm coming back, but as of now I'm retiring. I don't think I'll change my mind."

"Thank you so very much, Muhammad," said Hill. "And thank you from all of us from around the world."

"Thank you," said Ali, who cut a sorry figure as he climbed through the ropes, and started on the long journey back to the locker room, to the end of his career and the start of the rest of his life.

CHAPTER TWELVE
Farewell to the King

When I was twenty-six years old, I could chew up and spit out guys like Larry Holmes, Earnie Shavers, Gerrie Coetzee. But now I'm thirty-seven, and in a few weeks I could still whip them. But I don't want to kill myself training for 15 rounds. I have other battles to fight. My people want me to get out. I'd be a fool to fight again. As of now, I'm officially retired.

Muhammad Ali, Los Angeles, June 27, 1979

MUHAMMAD ALI SLUMPED ON A chair in the windowless locker-room of a municipal baseball field outside the town of Nassau. The white-washed walls were made of cinder blocks, the conditions were cramped, and the air reeked of sweat. A phalanx of sportswriters had pushed and shoved their way into a space so small it was agreed, only after some scuffles between heavy-handed security men and the fourth estate, that the journalists would come in and out in shifts. In this most unlikely of settings, they had come to record the last moments of the greatest of all boxing careers. They had come to hear the serial retirer say he was hanging them up for good. Once more with feeling.

"It's over," mumbled Ali. "It's over."

"No it ain't, champ, no it ain't," pleaded John Travolta, kneeling in front of his hero, sobbing at the sight of the boxer admitting to the journalists that this, indeed, was the end.

Outside, hundreds of fans, many of whom it turned out had been handed free tickets in hotel lobbies, were stopping on their way out of the venue to urinate against the outfield walls that had served as the male bathrooms for the evening.

"Everybody knew you won," whispered Veronica Ali to her husband.

On the other side of the wall, the cowbell that had been used to signal the start and end of rounds was being taken out, being returned to the farm from which it had come.

"You done good," said Herbert Muhammad. "I don't agree with that decision."

He hadn't done good. At all.

His newfound friend from Hollywood, his wife of four years, and his long-time manager were all lying. Maybe not lying. Perhaps just telling the vanquished fighter what they thought he wanted to hear.

"I don't want him to fight, but you people are brainwashing him into thinking he did badly against Berbick," said Veronica to reporters, admonishing them for their critiques. "You had made up your mind about the fight you were going to see before you saw it."

Ali knew better than that now. He had just spent most of ten rounds getting beaten up by Trevor Berbick, an inferior fighter twelve years his junior. His entourage may have wanted to continue promoting a delusion and/or soothing his ego, but the fifth defeat of his professional life had brought Ali belatedly to his senses.

"Father Time caught up with me," he said, the bombastic voice that often shook up the world now so faint as to be barely audible to the reporters leaning forward, still hanging on his every word. "I feel tired. Berbick was too strong, more aggressive. I just had the feeling I could do this thing. My mind said I'd do it. But I know I didn't have it out there. I did good for a thirty-nine-year-old, did all right considering I'll be forty in five weeks.

"I thought Berbick was shorter than he is. I didn't know he was so strong. He tagged me with a couple of hard ones and they tired me a bit. There's nothing to worry about. This is not going to bother me.

But I think it's too late to comeback. I always say that after fights these days. Who knows how I'll feel next week?"

After the first contingent of reporters had departed, and the second was about to be ferried in, Ali was helped up onto a rubbing table. When he saw him lying there, his eyes closed, his lips pursed, his body swaddled in blankets, Harold Conrad was reminded of a similar tableau in another locker room in the Philippines six years earlier.

"As I looked at Ali laid out, it hurt to realize that the rounds he had just fought were a tango compared to what he and Frazier had done to each other in Manila," wrote Conrad. "And here in Nassau, it was all he could have taken."

Others in the entourage were suffering, too. The sight of Ali losing like this had made Gene Kilroy's ulcers bleed and caused him to throw up blood.

Maryum Ali walked in, tears flowing down her face, and threw her arms around her father. "Don't cry, honey," he said. "It could have been worse."

Years later, she told Thomas Hauser of the moral quandary the bout had put her in.

"That was the only fight I wanted him to lose," she said. "I wanted him to win but I didn't, because if he won he'd keep fighting, and I didn't want him to fight anymore. I was in the last row of the first level of the stadium that night. And I remember saying to myself, 'If he loses, he won't fight again and I'll be happy. But if he wins, he'll go on and on.'"

Rasheda Ali was crying, too, while her twin Jamillah and Muhammad Jr. just looked unbearably sad. Then, Odessa Clay arrived and enveloped her boy in a mother's hug.

"You fought a good fight, son," she whispered. "I'm proud of you."

She was proud, but also happy his boxing career looked to be over.

"It was what he wanted to do, and he made millions of people happy," said Mrs. Clay. "I am just happy that he did not get hurt."

Her son remained philosophical as the questions kept coming.

"Berbick couldn't have beaten me if I wasn't thirty-nine years old," he said. "But I was thirty-nine."

James Cornelius, inevitably, viewed the whole night through his own unique prism, bizarrely regarding the abject performance as some sort of justification for dragging Ali here and subjecting him to this.

"In round one Ali threw more punches than he had in the entire fight against Holmes," wrote Cornelius. "I had proven my point. October tenth, 1980, Ali was sick, something was wrong. I had seen my hero fight a gallant battle, only to lose with unbearable pain. The critics had been right in their predictions of Ali's defeat, and the night and subsequent days were sheer sadness for me. The great gladiator had been humiliated for now, but America could be proud that he had attempted the impossible."

A question about Ali's future plans was first met with a reply that he'd need a few days to mull it over. Then he followed that up with a proper answer about wanting to be an Islamic preacher. When somebody asked whether he might be interested in becoming a goodwill ambassador or a peace envoy for the US government, he perked up, especially when it was suggested he could try to improve relations between Libya's Muammar Gaddhafi and the White House.

"Yes, I would like that," said Ali. "I have met him five times. It is hard for me to believe reports he is trying to have the president killed. I think that is propaganda."

Only Ali in the moments after his final fight, the waning minutes of his athletic career, could turn a press question about his retirement into a geo-political discussion about the concern that Libya was bent on assassinating Ronald Reagan. One more bizarre measure of the man. One more illustration of why so many journalists had made the trek to chronicle his demise, even in a place so ill-fitted to his stature.

"Graceful exits are rare in professional boxing, but few great champions have gone out more miserably..." wrote Hugh McIlvaney. "To see him lose to such a moderate fighter in such a grubby context was like watching a king ride into permanent exile on the back of a garbage truck. The one blessing was that he was steadily exhausted, rather than violently hurt by the experience."

Dick Young walked over and kissed Ali's face. Once one of his fiercest critics, perhaps his most trenchant media opponent for the longest time, this New York institution remained diametrically opposed to just about everything Ali had stood for. Yet, he had come to respect him enough that, here, in his final hour as a boxer, Young broke the fourth wall because he wanted or needed to embrace Ali as a way of acknowledging what he had meant to the sport and to the world, and to those fortunate enough to have tracked his remarkable journey.

"He'd taken us on the ride of our lifetimes," said Dave Kindred. "He was the greatest athlete we had ever seen or ever would see. Besides being the world's most famous man for much of the time, right there behind whoever happened to be the pope. Even if he fought again, I would not have been there. For long enough, I had seen him damage himself."

Others were having misgivings that they'd been lured to Nassau at all.

"Ali is my friend, although I have not seen or been with him for years," said Shelly Saltman. "I was extremely sad and sorry that I had been involved, even though my part I executed to the best of my ability. Ali was a shadow of himself, and as the fight wore on there were quite a few moments I felt like crying. Berbick did not hold back. He wanted to punish Ali and he wanted to win. Ali's tools had eroded. He was a shadow of the great fighter he had been. Doing this event was not enjoyable. I saw the demise of a fellow human being, and Muhammad was one that I loved and respected."

Beyond the Learesque portrait of Ali in the locker-room, the problems that had afflicted the promotion continued well into the Bahamian night. When Earnie Shavers heard Cornelius say he didn't have the money to pay the balance of his purse, the old heavyweight wasn't having it. He locked the door of the room they were standing in and told Cornelius that, unless he was Spider-Man, he wasn't leaving until the money was handed over. Victor Sayyah stepped in to make the shortfall appear from his magic suitcase, and Shavers was spared having to fight for the second time that evening.

Thomas Hearns had an even more pressing issue, a gaping wound that needed fixing before it blighted the rest of his career. Unfortunately, that kind of medical attention wasn't easily sourced in Nassau in the wee small hours of the morning. Emanuel Steward and Hearns toured the island in vain before returning to the Britannia Beach Hotel, where Angelo Dundee was standing in the lobby—still on duty.

"I heard you're trying to get someone for Tommy." said Dundee. "I've got a plastic surgeon friend of mine who traveled with me from Florida to take care of Ali in case Ali got cut. If you want, you can come up to my room and we'll see what we can do."

The facilities weren't what anybody was used to; a bedsheet was cut out in the shape of a face, but the need to be stitched up was, by that point, dire. So Dr. Julian Groff went to work without anesthetic, putting 121 stitches into Hearns as he lay there grimacing but never complaining. A bottle of whiskey was found and Steward, Dundee, and Dundee's wife Helen watched on, all three marveling at the lack of whining from the patient.

"I have never seen anybody as tough as this kid," said Groff.

In the departure lounge of Nassau Airport on Saturday, Tom Cushman ran into the Dundees, and they started to chat. Angelo confessed to having been very worried at the length of time between the final bell and the announcement of the judges' scorecards.

"I was afraid they were going to give him the decision," said Dundee.

"You mean Berbick?" asked Cushman.

"I mean Muhammad. If he wins, that means another fight. It's better this way."

Ali stayed in town on Saturday, and, in his remarkable way, opened the door of his villa to all comers. Harold Conrad and his wife, Mara, came to pay their respects and found the vanquished fighter in fine form given what had transpired. Conrad noticed now and again a faraway look in his old friend's eyes...at least until he decided he would entertain the gathering with a magic show so elaborate it formed the introduction for William Nack's evocative account in *Sports Illustrated* of what he'd witnessed during this bizarre interlude in the Bahamas.

"With his suit coat off and his tie loosened, Muhammad Ali perched on the edge of a couch in a villa in Nassau and for 40 minutes put on his most engaging entertainment of the week," wrote Nack. "'You want to see a magic show?' he had asked, opening up a black and red attache case. In the time it would take to go 10 rounds, the former heavyweight champion of the world turned half dollars into quarters and pennies into dimes, explaining the tricks as he went along. He made a small handkerchief and a candle disappear.

"He mysteriously transferred a foam rubber ball from his left hand to a guest's right. And he folded a silk hankie into quarters on the table and made it flutter up, phantomlike, as he chanted: 'Rise, ghost. Rise, ghost. Rise....' This was last Saturday afternoon and Ali's magic show stood as an ironic denouement to most of the preceding now-you-see-it, now-you-don't week. There was only one ghost in the Bahamas and it was Muhammad Ali, and the only magic he had left was that which he performed in his villa on—further irony—Paradise Island."

Earlier in the day, there'd been a formal press conference on the second floor of Loews Harbor Cove Hotel. Ali walked in, acknowledged all the familiar faces, then, with mischief in his eyes, made an announcement.

"Yes," he said. "I shall return . . . to Los Angeles, California."

The guffawing of fifty or so journalists filled the room and Ali, dramatic entrance now made, took a seat on the dais next to his conqueror.

"Beat up on an old man," said Ali, mock-taunting Berbick before eulogizing him. "The way I see it, Trevor is as good as any man I ever fought. I could hit Joe Frazier but I couldn't hit Trevor."

If that was an exaggeration of Berbick's true abilities, Ali was, during the ensuing question and answer session, actually in a very grounded place.

"What's it like to know that your skills may have gone?" went the question.

"They have gone," he answered. "Not *may* have gone. They have gone."

The events of the previous night had finally rid him of any delusions about where he stood. One slight bruise over his left eye aside, he sounded happy his final bout hadn't been marked by the type of ignominy and carnage often visited upon fighters who hang on way, way too long.

"I was lucky. No cuts, no bruises, no soreness. There was so much talk about me getting hurt. But I'm blessed. I didn't get disgraced. You might have seen me flat on my back, or slumped against the ropes, the referee pulling the man off of me."

More than one reporter present scribbled in his notebook that he'd said something identical after his defeat by Holmes in Las Vegas fourteen months before. And that was a commentary in itself on the unnecessarily elongated ending to his career. Then his opponent offered another.

"In the early rounds, I was trying to hit him on the chin and put him out of his misery," said Berbick. "I can't believe some of the shots he took. After a while I just wanted to throw enough punches to win. I didn't want to hit him hard, have him go down and not get back up."

Ali was gracious in his response to what was essentially a put-down.

"If he could have done any better, and didn't," he said, looking across at Berbick, "thank you."

After so much wishful thinking and a large dollop of fantasizing over the previous three months, Ali's tone was suddenly and refreshingly realistic. No more attempting to fool himself or everybody else.

"I'm not crazy. After Holmes, I had excuses. No excuses this time. I was in shape. My weight was right. I had ten rounds to do what I could do and I couldn't. I wasn't beat badly. I just couldn't do the things I wanted to do. I think I'm finished. I know it's the end."

When Berbick was asked what he had gleaned from this experience, Ali couldn't resist the chance to intervene, grabbing the microphone before saying, "He learned to retire before he gets to forty."

It was put to him that he might make good on an earlier promise to become a promoter, or stay in boxing in some other capacity. He shook his head. Perhaps chastened by the way his reputation had been traduced by Harold Smith and the mayhem that attended so much of the promotion in Nassau, this was no longer an appealing prospect.

"Doing that would be just like being an old-time fighter. Hanging around gyms. I don't want that type of image."

He didn't come across like somebody with a paucity of options or a need for money. He claimed, and there was no reason to doubt this, that he had been offered $10 million by one of the major oil corporations to become their corporate ambassador in the Middle East. Even if few would have been better equipped to deal with Islamic governments than the most famous Muslim on the planet, the role didn't interest him. He was more much more interested in the way he would now be perceived by fans.

"One good thing about losing the fight, people feel they're inferior when you're too good. But they know I can lose, too."

There was still time for reflection. Looking back, he reckoned his defeat of George Foreman in Zaire was his greatest fight, although he was "pretty good" against Joe Frazier in Manila, too. He joked that Frazier had phoned him already about the possibility of them going at it for a fourth time. Where? "In Harlem, in an alley."

At the end of the press conference, there was an extraordinary cameo. Ed Schuyler, the veteran boxing correspondent of the Associated Press, rose from his chair, and simply said, "Thanks for giving us one hell of a run."

It was a wonderful moment that captured the symbiotic relationship between the athlete and those who covered him over the previous twenty-one years. Of course, he couldn't resist puncturing the solemnity with humor.

"I don't know how I'll feel next month," he said, turning to Berbick and warning, "I'll get you next time."

When the laughter stopped, the emotions that many journalists felt at his departure were genuine. And the encomiums still needed to be written.

"You gave us twenty-one years of high excitement, bombast and poetry, controversy and drama, a lot of laughs and a ton of entertainment," wrote Will Grimsley, AP's special correspondent. "And you showed us the world—from Rome, where as a fat-faced light-heavyweight you won the Olympic gold medal to all those exotic places such as Kuala Lumpur, Zaire and Manila. No ocean was too wide to cross, no continent too remote to reach. You saw them all, hobnobbed with their presidents and potentates, and made the little people of the world feel like kings."

Red Smith put the end in some historical context.

"He was repetitious, boring, often entertaining, tireless, and the best thing that happened to boxing since Tom Sayers and John C. Heenan," wrote Smith, who called Ali's retirement the biggest sports event of 1981. "When Cassius was a youngster in Louisville, Ky., main-event fighters on Jim Norris's Friday night television shows received a TV fee of $1,000 each, in addition to the percentage of the live house negotiated with the promoter. When and if Gerry Cooney fights Larry Holmes March 15th, champion and challenger will get $10 million each. Muhammad Ali brought that change about."

Not all of the fall-out was so positive and complimentary.

Twenty-four hours after the fight, *Saturday Night Live's* Weekend Update featured a sports report in which Joe Piscopo interviewed Muhammad Ali, played by Eddie Murphy. The impression was, as usual, note perfect, but the script veered close to the bone.

Piscopo introduced the segment in the usual way that he parodied sportscasts, booming "The big story, Muhammad Ali! Last night... fight... drama... Bahama... LOST!" Then he showed some mock footage of him as a young journalist interviewing a twenty-year-old Cassius Clay, again expertly rendered by Murphy. However, the joke started to take on more of an edge when Piscopo cut to the present.

Like all the best satire, it was uncomfortable because it was so accurate. Murphy, as Ali, responded to some of the questions by stuttering and slurring unintelligibly, his mumbling greeted by peals of laughter from the in-studio audience. There was more guffawing when Ali responded to another query by launching into a rant in which it became obvious the befuddled boxer thought he was talking to Howard Cosell. The whole skit culminated in an exchange that would become an uncomfortable watch as the years wore on.

Piscopo: *Muhammad, are you gonna fight again?*

Ali: *I like your show, I admire your style, Old McDonald had a farm, eeh eye eeh eye oh...and on this farm he had some...*

Piscopo: *There you have it. [Audience erupts again.] Ali confused, career over, brain cells few. Joe Piscopo, live Saturday night sports.*

By the following Tuesday, Ali was back home in Los Angeles where he gave an interview to Jim Hill of KNXT-TV, the local CBS affiliate in Los Angeles. Before the cameras even started rolling at his home in Hancock Park, he assured Hill he had a big story for him. Despite the fact his retirement had been widely reported every day since the fight, and the tributes were still taking up column inches in newspapers, he hinted at yet another about-turn.

"I'm still thinking. I haven't made my mind up yet."

Why the change of heart so quickly? Well, he claimed to have received a phone call from an individual who had spoken at length to the judges after the fight. New information had come to light, making him rethink his decision to hang up his gloves.

"They said if I won the fight, they knew I would have kept going," said Ali. "Public sentiment, the people are all wishing I would quit. They knew if I would win I would go on further. So to save me and protect me, they gave it to Berbick, hoping I would stop. Now that I have found that out, they have encouraged me to go on in the future. If I want it to happen, it will happen. We'll see. The reflexes are gone, the speed is gone, the strength is gone. Maybe I'm going to show you it's not."

Hill, a former NFL player, had been part of the commentary team for the fight. He'd witnessed the beating Ali had taken. Before the interview, he'd warned Ali if he started talking about continuing to fight he was going to call him out for being crazy. And he did. But Ali tried to convince him that the loss had been painless.

"I know myself," he said. "I wasn't hurt. I'm not getting hurt. I was off for a year. I'll tell you when I'm through. How can I be through? Look at me. Do I look like I'm finished? I don't want to make excuses but I barely trained for the fight against Berbick. My reflexes and timing wasn't what it should be. I need more training. I have a couple of men in the top ten and we have a license in another country. We don't need this country because they will say no."

Within hours, Angelo Dundee and Howard Bingham were denying that Ali had any notion of coming back, claiming he'd only been kidding around with Hill.

"He won't fight again," said Dundee. "I think I said the thing that would beat him was the grind and it did. I'm very happy it ended up like it did. It was the best thing he could do."

The reporter, however, stood by his story.

"There's no way he was kidding," said Hill. "At least at that time, he was serious."

He may have been in earnest, but nobody else could take the idea seriously. For one very simple reason. There was just no money to be made from another Ali fight.

"The public just wouldn't pay to see him anymore, and no one knows better than Ali that that's the bottom line in the fight racket," wrote Harold Conrad. "It didn't really matter that he wasn't the fighter he once was. He wasn't the draw, and that was that. The so-called promoters of the Bahama fight scaled the house to start at $1,000 for ringside seats. Add up your fingers and toes and you have more digits than the number of $1,000 seats they sold. Then they dropped the price to $500, and Kojak's got more hairs on his head than the number of $500 seats they sold. They were lucky they had 10,000, and that was counting the guys who jumped over the fence and got in for free."

Almost exactly twelve months later, Ali arrived in the United Arab Emirates to fight three exhibition matches in a week. The third of those had to be canceled due to poor ticket sales.

"It would be a rank injustice to a great boxer," said a spokesman for the organizers, "to make him work hard without having anyone appreciate it."

CHAPTER THIRTEEN
Of Gods and Monsters

This fight will let the world know that I'm back. I'm sharp and I'm better than I was twenty years ago. The Lord has done that to me, just as He promises to renew anybody who praises and worships Him and lifts up Hs name. When people see me they're going to see a living miracle. They're going to say: "How can a man who's forty years old function like he's eighteen or nineteen?"

Trevor Berbick, Miami, August 1994

ON NOVEMBER 22, 1986, THE Las Vegas Hilton hosted the fifth instalment in HBO's eight-bout series designed to unify the heavyweight division, a clash between WBC champion Trevor Berbick and the challenger, Mike Tyson. With a record of 27 wins, including 25 by knockout (fifteen of those coming in the first round), and no losses, Tyson was the real box office draw that night. Just twenty years old, he had electrified the entire sport with his curt and savage dismissals of so many opponents over the previous year and a half, and this, finally, represented his chance to grab a piece of the heavyweight crown that many believed it was his destiny to hold.

Muhammad Ali was in town for the occasion, typically attracting huge crowds every time he walked through the Hilton lobby, and before the bell he visited the young contender. When the once and future champions embraced, Ali whispered in Tyson's ear, "Kick his ass for me!" As if the phenom needed any further encouragement to visit destruction on any quarry. Almost five full years had passed since Berbick had defeated him in that baseball field in the Bahamas, but Ali obviously hadn't forgotten.

For his own part, Berbick's circuitous and eventful journey to the showdown with Tyson that was billed as "Judgement Day" had been a long and very, very strange trip.

Six months after Nassau, Berbick pounded his way to a convincing victory over the higher-ranked and previously undefeated Greg Page on the undercard of Holmes's title defense against Gerry Cooney. If that type of result and performance lent credibility to his burgeoning claims to be a genuine contender, his next outing against Renaldo Snipes was a very different affair.

By the time he arrived at the Sands Hotel and Casino in Atlantic City, New Jersey, in October 1982, Berbick's affairs were being looked after by Herbert Muhammad, Ali's longtime manager. Less than a year after they were on opposite sides in the Bahamas, this relationship appeared to further the prevailing view that this was a fighter on the way up—which he definitely was, until a bizarre series of unfortunate events that evening.

The drama began when Berbick threatened to pull out just hours before the first bell in a dispute over the size of the purse. He thought he was fighting for $300,000. Don King Productions, which was promoting the event, told him he'd signed on for half that. The arguing became so intense that, ninety minutes before fight time, nobody was sure there'd even be a bout. Eventually, belatedly, Berbick, looking flabbier around the middle than at any point in the previous years, made his way to the ring.

Perhaps predictably, Snipes started much the brighter, putting Berbick down with a magnificent right in the first and looking better in the early rounds. Even if he couldn't keep up that breakneck pace, Snipes inflicted enough damage in the first half of a contest that went ten rounds to gain a deserved decision. In the aftermath, Berbick gave his excuse.

"I've been victimized," he said. "I was really pressured about four hours before the fight, and it really drained my energy."

That much was true. The ridiculous nature of the last-minute purse negotiations would have drained anybody. However, later he concocted a different version of this story, alleging that something altogether more sinister was afoot.

"They tried to kill me," said Berbick. "They drugged me. But it wasn't strong enough; it didn't affect me."

Seven months on, his comeback bout was against S. T. Gordon, a journeyman cruiserweight who hadn't fought in this division for five years. At the Showboat in Las Vegas on a card televised nationally by ABC, Berbick stunk up the joint for the first eight rounds, appearing wholly disinterested and barely throwing punches. Then, obviously realizing how far behind he was on the judges' scorecards, he finally roused himself into action in the ninth. Too little, too late. Another defeat for his résumé and the birth of one more colorful conspiracy theory. This time, he claimed some bad people who wanted to become his managers had plotted to poison him.

"They tried everything in the book to get rid of me," he said. "They knew that I liked watermelon and fruit. They put it in there. Somebody gave me something that stopped my body functioning. I knew something was wrong before the fight. I was like a mummy. I couldn't move. I found out who did it, but I won't say who."

An unfortunate pattern had begun to develop that would mark the remainder of Berbick's career and life. To explain away embarrassing defeats or (later) serious crimes, he would offer increasingly ridiculous and odd explanations. At first these sorts of inventions stretched credulity and merely amused the press. Eventually, they led many to question his sanity, and to ponder the deleterious impact of taking too many blows to the head.

Regardless of his tendency towards fantastical excuses, his career was going nowhere by the summer of 1983. Closing in on thirty years of age (if not there already), two consecutive and mediocre losses had him sliding down the rankings, and his prospects never looked bleaker. Yet, to his credit, he kept fighting. The purses became smaller, the coverage minuscule compared to the Ali and Holmes bouts. But, somehow, he recovered his mojo, winning eight in a row over the next three years in venues all over America and as far afield as London, England. Along the way, he started a family with his new wife, Nadine (he had two kids from a previous relationship in Canada), and relocated to Florida.

The victories were good for padding his record, but the caliber of opponents did little for his reputation as an eminently beatable fighter. Again, strangely, this negative can turn into a positive for a fighter seeking work. Having the reputation of somebody who can be defeated will always earn you a shot at the title. So it proved in March 1986, when Berbick was lined up to take on Pinklon Thomas in the first fight of HBO's ambitious series to unify the division. Thomas had held the WBC belt since 1984, and for him Berbick looked to be a perfect fit, a credible opponent who didn't pose too much real danger of wresting away his crown. Or so the self-managed Thomas, with an unblemished 27 and 0 record, thought.

"Well, there was no empiric science of analyzing the mind of a fighter," wrote the late Phil Berger in his classic book, *Blood Season*. "But in the days before the fight, Thomas provided a pretty fair clue that he might not be taking Berbick all that seriously. In the lobby of the Riviera Hotel and Casino, he spent hours selling audio cassettes of himself crooning an easy listening ballad written for him called 'Hanging on to Promises'."

During the buildup, Thomas also regaled reporters about his elaborate future plans to juggle a singing career with managing his own stable of fighters.

Just 2,000 people paid into the hotel ballroom for a contest in which Berbick was a six-and-a-half-to-one underdog. He later admitted to being so taken with the odds he was tempted to bet half of his $50,000 purse on the outcome.

"But I'm a soldier of Christ," he said, "I couldn't do that."

Given that Thomas was guaranteed $635,000 for his night's work, it would be convenient to surmise Berbick's greater hunger, not to mention his canny decision to start working with Eddie Futch beforehand, gave him a decided advantage. In fact, Thomas contributed just as much to an excellent contest that one reporter described as "a war of attrition."

In the eleventh round, Berbick, ahead on points, appeared set to finish the affair. He rocked Thomas with a left hook, but somehow the champion stayed upright, withstood a subsequent barrage and hung in there for one more round. It didn't matter in the end. All three judges scored it in favor of the challenger. Improbably, he now held the WBC belt. Even in the alphabet soup of modern boxing, he could call himself a genuine world heavyweight champion.

"I say this to you," said Berbick during his post-fight interview. "That many people don't understand what mysteries I've been through. But I think right after this fight, and pretty soon.... I won't say too much, but where I build my church and the gates of heaven, hell will not prevail against it. You don't understand that. People will understand it soon."

Even as the press lapped up enigmatic quotes of that caliber, and photographers snapped him celebrating in the ring with his son Trevor Jr., Berbick's affairs were actually in a bit of a mess. The professional relationship with Herbert Muhammad having proved short-lived, he was now managing and promoting himself. Which may explain why, after the fight, the Nevada State Athletic Commission held on to his purse. Two rival promoters claimed he owed them part of the money for bouts he'd signed on to and pulled out of. This type of snafu was to become a recurring motif as his career wore on.

Still, in the short term his achievement afforded him a soapbox like never before, and he was happy to use it.

"First, I'm going to destroy all the devils—I mean the fighters—who stand between me and the unified heavyweight championship of the world," he assured the *Toronto Star*. "Then I'm coming home. God raised me up for a purpose! I'm here, God! I know that now. This is His way of letting me show the world. I'm coming home, to Canada. People up there, they love me, I love them. I want to let the kids know what life is all about. I want to make them proud. God brought me to Canada to lead the children! I will go all across the country talking to them. I will instruct them, I will lead them in Christ! They're the greatest asset Canada has. I'm here to motivate them, I'm here to teach them, I'm here to love them!"

There was also recognition from unlikely quarters. In Miramar, South Florida, where he now made his home, April 7, 1986 was declared Trevor Berbick Day. At a meeting in City Hall, he was besieged by fans and honored with the key to the city. The mayor paid him fulsome tribute and the boxer repaid the compliments.

"This is a wonderful city to live in," Berbick said. "I especially want to thank the police officers who cheer me on. They are all very understanding when they see me out running along the roadside in the early hours of the morning."

A decade after moving to Canada in pursuit of a boxing career, Berbick had finally reached the big time. In June, he sat down with Dennis Rappaport, co-manager of Gerry Cooney, to discuss the possibility of meeting the man then trading as the latest great white hope. There followed a conversation that would become part of Berbick's legend.

"I need money, a $100,000 deposit," said Berbick.

"What?" asked Rappaport.

"I got a message from God. He said to ask you, and you'd give it to me."

"When did you speak to God?"

"About twenty minutes ago."

"Trevor," said Rappaport. "He changed his mind. He spoke to me about five minutes ago and said not to give you $20."

The fight never happened. By then, Berbick was being advised by a Jamaican businessman named Lucien Chen, whose interests include a chain of legal bookmakers in Kingston and a video rental store in Miami. Over the course of that summer, the pair of them played off the possibility of a clash with Cooney against a proposed meeting with

Mike Tyson, all the while trying to increase the purse on offer. There ensued rounds of intense negotiations in Las Vegas, encounters chronicled in forensic detail by Phil Berger in *Blood Season*.

During this series of increasingly frenetic and bad-tempered contract discussions, Berbick often cut a strange figure. It was not unusual for him to talk to himself as lawyers for both sides threw numbers and conditions back and forth. One attorney recalled a meeting in which the boxer passed the time autographing a box of identical photographs of himself, picking each one up, holding it close to his face, and examining it minutely before writing his name across it and putting it back in the pile.

After more bargaining in Las Vegas in September, and many more screaming matches, Don King finally convinced Berbick to take the Tyson fight for a fee of $2.1 million. That one-third of the sum was going to be paid to King's son, Carl Jr.—now also Berbick's sometime manager—captures the nature of a rather convoluted and corrupt arrangement.

Tyson-Berbick wasn't just one of the biggest fights of the year, it was one of the most eagerly-awaiting sporting events. And that meant the spotlight on both combatants was far more intense than usual. Tyson didn't need much advance billing; the savage manner of his victories and his rapid rise ensured that. But Berbick was being introduced to the wider American public as "The Fighting Preacher." Always an easy sell.

Journalists in town to cover Tyson's presumed coronation lapped up stories of Berbick's faith, all the more so because it allowed them to offer such a stark contrast between the boxers. The unrepentant *enfant terrible* from Brooklyn in one corner, a recently ordained minister from Las Vegas' Moments of Miracles Tabernacle in the other.

Don King, of course, did much to burnish the halo over Berbick's head. He told a tale of how, during an especially dark time in his own life, when the government was investigating him for tax evasion, this fighter with whom he had a tumultuous and distrustful relationship had tried to provide succor to the beleaguered promoter.

"Every morning at 6:30 a.m. there'd be a knock on my hotel door," King said, "and here would come Trevor Berbick, carrying a Bible and a cross. 'While everybody may be your enemy, the Lord is on your side,' he'd tell me. I'd be sleepy and half groggy while he'd preach. Two, three weeks in a row, he'd be there first thing in the morning, reading the 91st Psalm: 'He that dwelleth in the secret place of the most High shall abide under. . . .' "

For his part, Berbick announced his intention to write a book about his extraordinary life, and reiterated that he was going to use his status as champion and the accompanying wealth for a higher purpose.

"I'm building a ministry and I'm building a beautiful career, and it couldn't have happened to a more deserving guy," he said. "The beauty of my ministry is that I won't need no money from people. I preach in my room. I preach to my sparring partners. I love everybody."

Of course, the reality of his life was a little more hectic than he was letting on. When leaving Johnny Tocco's gym at Main and Charleston after a sparring session a few days before the Tyson fight, a process server chased Berbick across the car park, flinging a writ at him. A Texas promoter wanted $495,000 from his $2.1 million purse, claiming the money was owed to him by Berbick for pulling out of a fight with Tony Perea back in 1982.

Taking time out for a court appearance perhaps wasn't the best preparation for fighting a man bent on becoming the youngest champion in history. On top of that, the fact Berbick couldn't reach financial terms with Futch this time around meant he also had to switch trainers. Even if Angelo Dundee—another throwback to that night in Nassau—was a worthy replacement, arriving in town two and a half weeks before the fight added to the impression that Berbick's camp was rather chaotic.

"But if he's the same Trevor Berbick who fought Pinklon Thomas, he'll do a number on Tyson," said Dundee, dutifully earning his corn in the pre-fight interview. "Berbick is the best fighter Tyson ever fought. I found out Berbick's an athlete. When he goes home to Jamaica, he runs with Don Quarrie, their Olympic gold-medal winner. And he's got good balance. He don't look it because he's blocky, but he's balanced."

In a backhanded tribute to his improved standing, *Ring* magazine did caution: "Berbick is the kind of fighter who wins when you least expect him to."

Tyson's gospel all that week was of a very different timbre. He was a lot less talkative around reporters. And when he did speak, he sounded like a man readying himself for war, explaining that his unwillingness to show emotion was part of his professional mien, and ominously declaring the title at stake as a "crown reserved for men only." When asked about the threat Berbick posed, Tyson dismissed the suggestion: "He has nothing to fight me with."

That would prove scarily close to the truth. When the bell rang, Tyson seemed determined to honor Ali's pre-fight wish, going on the offensive immediately, and, defying all predictions, Berbick neither ran nor tried to get in close and hold on. Instead, he stood and fought. Or, at least, he tried to fight in the face of a sustained onslaught throughout a thrilling yet one-sided first round.

"My punches," said Tyson later, "had murderous intentions. I was throwing hydrogen bombs."

Somehow, Berbick managed to survive until the bell, then he stuck his tongue out at Tyson, arguably the most defiant gesture he'd make all night. In Berbick's corner, Dundee was furious. The crowd might have been loving the all-action approach, but he was apoplectic at the way in which his charge had chosen to battle.

"What are you doing?" he roared. "You're fighting his fight. Go out there and do your own thing."

During the second round, the hammering continued. At ringside, Nadine Berbick's face betrayed the suffering and concern of a woman witnessing her spouse being assaulted. As the crowd grew noisier and noisier, sensing the end was nigh, they drowned out the sound of her plaintively calling out her husband's name.

It had already become a case of when, not if, Tyson would win. With two minutes and thirty-five seconds gone in the second, referee Mills Lane ended Berbick's suffering after a left hook to the temple turned his legs to rubber. Valiantly though he tried to get back up, he staggered around the ring, repeatedly falling like a drunk groping for a bar stool that remained tantalizingly out of reach.

There was no shame in losing to Tyson in his prime, even in a tragi-comic manner that would make the culmination of the fight a YouTube staple decades later. And immediately afterwards, Berbick spoke graciously in defeat, acknowledging the speed and power of the punches that he'd taken. He even admitted how naïve he'd been to think he could go toe to toe with the challenger. However, with time, it became apparent that he lost a lot more than just a title that night. In search of a way to explain the beating he took, he headed down an all too familiar and very dark path.

"When the bell rang after the first round and I went to my corner, they did something, they put something in my water," claimed Berbick later. "They gave me a drink with something. They put something in my nose. Something. It's obvious."

Aside from claiming that antibiotics he took for a cold affected his equilibrium during the contest, he also alleged that those who wanted him to lose that evening had earlier pumped some sort of damaging gas into his hotel room as he slept. It wasn't the first time he'd made that type of accusation. Indeed, thirteen years later, he'd calmly explain to a reporter that he always went to bed with the windows in his room open just in case somebody tried the same ruse again.

This all might have been dismissed as the quirky excuse-making of a fighter determined to convince himself he wasn't simply outclassed, except that by now this was his go-to way of explaining when things went wrong inside and outside the ring. And, unfortunately, his career was going to head pretty much downhill from that point on.

"Fighting is something that I want to do now," said Berbick before he fought John Tate back in 1980. "I don't want to be hanging on when I'm thirty-five. I want to prove some things to myself. I want to use this as a way to reach people. And it can be economically successful. But I don't really like boxing."

Two decades after he uttered those words, Berbick (officially forty-six, unofficially who knows?) climbed through the ropes for his last competitive bout in Vancouver. By then, his name was so tarnished, so associated in the public mind with criminality and law-breaking that, for a time, he'd even fought as Israel T. Berbick. If the idea was to try to get away from his past, well, that was impossible because his charge sheet by then was too long and too tawdry.

His legal troubles began in earnest in 1990 when there was a litany of cases in which he was the defendant. First, he was charged with aggravated assault after an incident with a man he suspected was having an affair with his wife. Then, he was picked up for fraud for securing a mortgage for $90,000 against the family home in Miramar by having a woman pose as his wife.

As that year drew to a close, he was arrested in Miami for putting a gun to the neck of Novelette Hanse, his former money manager. Accusing her of stealing $40,000 from him, he also demanded she drive him to see his by-then estranged wife. When he missed a court date in relation to that case, he ended up in jail for eight days before the trial. While a Broward County jury eventually acquitted him of the more serious charge of kidnapping, they found him guilty of simple misdemeanor assault and he was sentenced to six months' probation.

"The world is going to see Trevor Berbick come back," he told reporters outside the court. "All this makes me so much stronger, mentally and physically. I've been training hard in jail."

In April 1991, forty-one-year-old Larry Holmes won a comeback bout against Tim "Doc" Anderson at the Diplomat Hotel and Resort in Hollywood, Florida, and Berbick turned up at the post-fight press conference. He apparently took offense when Holmes dismissed a reporter's suggestion that the two former heavyweight champions might reprise their 1981 meeting in Las Vegas. After Holmes departed the conference room, Berbick began ranting about how his former opponent had been responsible for the breakup of his marriage, and threatened a street fight in which he'd break all the ribs in Holmes's body.

"He used his sweetheart to mess up my married life!" said Berbick, wearing a sharp suit and tie. "Jenny from Jacksonville. I got proof and tapes. All the problems I have are through him. My kids are suffering, too."

When word of these accusations reached Holmes elsewhere in the building, he went looking for retribution. He found Berbick in front of the hotel and set about him, kicking and punching repeatedly until police eventually separated the two men.

"Larry Holmes punched me," screamed Berbick, as two cops tried to lead him away from the scene. "Everybody saw him kick and punch me."

As he finished that sentence, Holmes, still in his white tracksuit, re-appeared. He ran across the roofs of two parked cars and then flung himself through the air at Berbick. Mayhem ensued.

No charges arose out of that incident, but the footage made a laughingstock of two fighters whose best days were now long gone. Being a figure of ridicule, though, was the least of Berbick's issues.

In 1992, he was found guilty of sexual battery of a twenty-six-year-old woman who had babysat his kids. The assault took place at the woman's Fort Lauderdale home, and in court she spoke for ninety minutes about her ordeal at his hands. It also emerged that in the 1980s, he'd been acquitted of the rape of a sixteen-year-old girl in Halifax.

In the Florida case, he refused to accept any culpability.

"Hey, I'm not an abusive person," said Berbick. "I didn't hurt that girl. She knows this. My wife got upset and didn't know what she wanted to do, so she told a lie."

Sentencing had to be delayed because Judge Thomas Wilson ordered a psychiatric evaluation of Berbick, who had been a restless and outspoken presence in the courtroom, often pacing up and down with his arms in the air. Several times, he had to be cautioned about his behavior, including one outburst in which he accused the victim of being "on the payroll," and another that saw him blame the situation on "secret agents."

"He sees himself as somewhat invulnerable," testified psychiatrist Sanford Jacobson. "His defeats are not really defeats. His knockouts are not really knockouts."

When the sentence was finally announced, Berbick roared at his wife, Nadine, and his attorney, accusing them of plotting against him. "You know what you did, God will punish you."

He also went into a rant about how the whole farrago had been a conspiracy involving Larry Holmes, Don King, and the Japanese. (A year earlier, he had fought Nobuhiko Takada in a ludicrous boxer-ver-sus-wrestler bout in Tokyo.)

"It is painful, but there's not much I can do," said Nadine Berbick outside the court, as the family began to speculate about whether too many blows to the head had contributed to his deterioration. "I know that I'm not hurting him. I testified for him at the sentencing."

Even more portentous was the comment of his lawyer, Mark Panunzio: "It's really hard when a client turns on you like this. You don't know what this cost me. This case wasn't done for the money. Trevor doesn't have a dime."

He served fifteen months of his sentence, and on release began working out at the 35th Street Gym in Miami, where he met Sergeant Patrick Burns, a trainer who helped him restart his career.

"Joseph went to prison for two years, and came out to be governor of Egypt," said Berbick in March 1994, blithely comparing his conviction to the suffering of a slave in the Book of Genesis. "I think I've been blessed tremendously. I feel like I'm nineteen or twenty years old again. The world is going to be surprised when they see me. I'm sharp and I'm better than I was twenty years ago. The Lord has done that to me, just as He promises to renew anybody who praises and worships Him and lifts up His name."

Three years after defeating Garing Lane on points at the Palais des Festivals in Cannes, France, Berbick was the headliner in a Toughman night of fighting in Spartanburg, South Carolina, boxing's equivalent of a former Major Leaguer turning up in single A ball in the boon-docks. Yet, as so often in the Berbick story, he kept going, most likely because he had no other way of turning a buck.

Despite the criminal record, there were always promoters willing to put him on the bill. Why? Well, aside from having fought seven world champions, he had a unique calling card. He was the only active fighter in the world who could claim a victory over Ali and a defeat against

Tyson (even if by that point he was claiming the devastating left hook to the temple actually missed, and the fight was fixed).

In 1999, Berbick, still wearing a jacket that had "WBC World Heavyweight Champion" emblazoned across the shoulders, turned back the clock and defeated Shane Sutcliffe, twenty-one years his junior, at the Centre Pierre Charbonneau in Montreal. He took home $10,000 and was crowned Canadian heavyweight champion again. Nearly a quarter of a century after first meeting him, Taylor Gordon and his son, Wayne, worked his corner that night. It was a last-minute favor. They were actually in the arena because one of their own fighters was on the undercard.

Immediately afterwards, Berbick delivered a familiar spiel, thanking his God and predicting this would be the springboard to launch him back to the top of the sport and towards millions of dollars in future earnings. The reality of what came after was very different. Less than a year later, a CAT scan revealed a blood clot on his brain and his license to box was revoked. His latest brush with fame had also brought him to the attention of federal authorities, who began deportation proceedings against him.

Although he won the right to stay in Canada for five more years because, among other things, young boxers testified that he was an inspiration to them in the gym, his press clippings from that time are typically troubling.

Witness this account of God visiting him in his apartment.

"I couldn't see His face. I'm always catching the back of the man, just His shoulders and head. Ghosts don't operate like that. I knew it was the Son of Man because the same thing happened to Moses. I'm a biblical historian. I'm deep."

Or his reaction to the initial threat of being sent out of the country.

"No one can move me from Montreal because God wants me here. People have got to be careful because God will take revenge against them."

By December 2002, he was back living in Florida. There, a routine traffic stop led the authorities to discover he had violated the conditions of his parole—enough of a transgresssion for them to start deportation proceedings. Trouble followed him back home to Jamaica. Not long after arriving, he went on the lam after being accused of larceny and housebreaking.

Facing charges relating to the theft of a television and a stereo from a house in his hometown of Port Antonio, he told police that somebody else had broken into his home and stashed the stolen goods there when he was away at the beach. It was another to add to the constantly growing list of cases against him, and worrying evidence that returning to live in the place of his birth for the first time in nearly four decades was never going to bring him the peace he sought.

Epilogue

TREVOR BERBICK SPENT THE LAST night of his life socializing. He attended a party at Miss Dorraine's Bar in Norwich, where he ate bread and chicken and danced enthusiastically to World Beat music, some of the selections there being made by his nephew, Harold. Shortly before midnight, he ended up at McCarthy's Bar. There, he made small talk with the bartender, Christine Davis, then sat at the end of the counter and watched television. He was a regular in the establishment, though staff never remembered seeing him drinking heavily nor causing trouble in any way.

He left McCarthy's around 1:00 a.m. on Saturday and started to walk back to his mother's house in Norwich, the place he now called home. Since returning to Jamaica, he'd had his share of problems: squabbles with his family and run-ins with the law. Yet earlier that month he'd given an interview to a local paper in which he sounded optimistic about his future. He'd fallen back in love with fishing, claimed to have plans to develop some property, and dreamt of opening a gym to coach youngsters. He was even in the market for a screenwriter to pitch Hollywood the story of his extraordinary life.

As was his custom when he neared home, Berbick took a short cut through the Church of God premises, using his cell phone to illuminate a path. At this hour of the night, however, it was still dark enough for two men to be lurking in the shadows, wielding a crowbar and a four-foot-long metal pipe, waiting for his arrival.

"He was coming up the church steps mumbling," said twenty-year-old Harold Berbick, one of the assailants, in a statement to police. "He had a phone in his hand with the light turn on when him pass me. He could not see us and I use the piece of iron to lick him in his head back twice. I was aiming for his neck and shoulder but it catch him in his head. He held his head with both hands and bend forward and Sheldon [nickname of the co-accused, eighteen-year-old Kenton Gordon] use the crowbar and hit him two times in his head also. Uncle Trevor drop to the ground and try to bawl out in a low voice and tried to get up but when he was getting up Sheldon hit him in his head two more times and he dropped to the ground."

The post-mortem examination revealed that Trevor Berbick died due to massive brain damage and hemorrhaging caused by repeated blows to the head by blunt objects. The coroner estimated that his death occurred within half an hour of him being first struck.

Harold Berbick had no previous convictions. During the trial, he claimed he was afraid of his uncle, and that at Miss Dorraine's on the night of October 27 he had made threatening gestures towards him from across the room, including repeatedly dragging a finger across his throat. The pair had a long-standing acrimonious relationship, and there had also been a violent incident between Harold's mother, Gwendolyn Facey, and Trevor earlier in the year, about which a case had been pending.

On December 20, 2007, a jury took just over an hour to find Harold guilty of murder; he was sentenced to life with a recommendation he spend at least twenty years in jail. Kenton Gordon was convicted of manslaughter, for which he received fourteen years hard labor.

"It is wrong to murder someone, justice has been served," said Berbick's ex-wife, Nadine, who had sat through the proceedings with two of his daughters, Trisha and Nadia. "He should not have died the way he did."

Sources

Select Bibliography

Allison, Dean and Henderson, Bruce B. *Empire of Deceit: Inside the Biggest Sports and Bank Scandal in History*. Doubleday, New York, 1985

Berger, Phil. *Blood Season*. Queen Anne Press, London, 1989

Berger, Phil. *Punch Lines: Berger on Boxing*. Four Walls Eight Windows, New York, 1993

Conrad, Harold. *Dear Muffo*. Stein and Day, New York, 1982

Cornelius, James. *The Last Punch*. General Publishing, Atlanta, 1985

Cushman, Tom. *Muhammad Ali and the Greatest Heavyweight Generation*. South East Missouri State University Press, Cape Girardeau, 2009

Dundee, Angelo. *I Only Talk Winning*. Contemporary Books, Chicago, 1985

Early, Gerard. *I'm a Little Bit Special*. Yellow Jersey Press, London, 1999

Early, Gerard. *The Culture of Bruising*. Ecco Press, New Jersey, 1994

Ehrenfeld, Rachel. *Evil Money – Encounters Along the Money Trail.* Harper Business, New York, 1992

Gorn, Elliot J. *Ali: The People's Champ.* University of Illinois Press, Chicago, 1995

Hannigan, Dave. *The Big Fight.* Yellow Jersey Press, London, 2002

Hauser, Thomas. *Muhammad Ali – His Life and Times.* Pan Books, London, 1992

Hughes, Brian and Hughes, Damian, *Hit Man: The Thomas Hearns Story.* Milo Books, England, 2010

Jones, Chris. *Falling Hard.* Arcade Publishing, New York, 2002

Kindred, Dave. *Heroes, Fools & Other Dreamers.* Longstreet Press, Atlanta, 1988

Kindred, Dave. *Sound and Fury.* Simon and Schuster, New York, 2006

Lyons, Thomas and Saltman, Shelly. *Fear No Evel.* We Publish Books, Rancho Mirage, 2007

McIlvanney, Hugh. *McIlvanney on Boxing.* Beaufort Books, New York, 1982

Newfield, Jack. *Only in America – The Life and Crimes of Don King.* William Morrow, New York, 1995

O'Brien, Pat. *I'll Be Back Right After This.* St. Martin's Press, New York, 2014

Pacheco, Ferdie. *The Fight Doctor.* Birch Lane Press, New York, 1992

Pacheco, Ferdie. *Tales from the Fifth Street Gym*. University Press of Florida, Gainesville, 2010

Parkinson, Michael. *Parky's People*. Hodder, London, 2011

Reed, Ishmael. *The Complete Muhammad Ali*. Baraka Books, Montreal, 2015

Schulberg, Budd. *Loser and Still Champion*. Doubleday, New York, 1972

Shavers, Earnie. *Welcome to the Big Time*. Sports Publishing, Illinois, 2002

Smith, Gary. *Going Deep*. Sports Illustrated Books, New York, 2002

Strathmore, William. *Muhammad Ali – The Unseen Archives*. Paragon, Bath, 2001

Stravinsky, John. *Muhammad Ali*. Park Lane Press, New York, 1997

Tanner, Michael. *Ali in Britain*. Mainstream, Edinburgh, 1995

Taylor, Jim. *Forgive Me My Press Passes*. Horsdal and Schubart, Victoria, 1993

Torres, José. *Sting Like a Bee*. Abelard Schuman, New York, 1971

West, David. *The Mammoth Book of Muhammad Ali*. Constable and Robinson, London, 2012

Newspapers and Periodicals

Chicago Sun-Times, Chicago Tribune, Detroit Free Press, Eugene Register-Guard, The Guardian, Jamaica Gleaner, Jamaica Observer, Lakeland Ledger, Las Vegas Sun, Los Angeles Times, Milwaukee Journal, Montreal Gazette, Nassau Guardian, New Straits Times, New York magazine,

New York Daily News, New York Times, The Observer, Ocala Star-Banner, Ottawa Citizen, Palm Beach Post, Philadelphia Daily News, Reading Eagle, Rolling Stone, Sarasota Journal, Spartanburg Herald-Journal, Spokesman Review, Sport, Sports Illustrated, St. Petersburg Independent, Sumter Daily Item, The Sun-Sentinel, The Times, Toronto Globe and Mail, Washington Post

Interviews
Allen Abel, Steve Bezanson, Michael Farber, Dave Kindred, Stone McEwan, Shelly Saltman

Television
"*Saturday Night Live*," NBC, December 12, 1981

Websites
http://www.boxingscene.com/trevor-berbick-part-history–6037
http://www.courtofappeal.gov.jm/sites/default/files/judgments/Berbick%20(Harold)%20and%20Gordon%20(Kenton)%20v%20R.pdf
http://www.livefight.com/news.php?news_id=3017&y=2013&m=07
http://blog.gitmomemory.org/2012/08/06/jamaican-workers/
http://fivedogs.tripod.com/shavers.html
http://forum.philboxing.com/viewtopic.php?f=5&t=10341
http://www.secondsout.com/ringside/a-fighters-perspective/eddie-gregory–the-fighter

Index